Natural Small Batch Cheesemaking

Kate Downham

Copyright ©2023 Kate Downham
All rights reserved.

All pictures copyright Kate Downham, except for the ruminant stomach diagram on page 25, from the public domain.

ISBN 978-0-6484661-9-2

www.thenourishinghearthfire.com

Other books by Kate Downham:
Backyard Dairy Goats
A Year in an Off-Grid Kitchen

eBooks by Kate Downham:
How to Start a Bulk Food Pantry on a Budget
Grain-Free Sweets and Treats
How to Create a Resilient Off-Grid Home
A Guide to Buy It Once Cookware

For my ancestors, and my children.

Thank you!

My name is on the cover of this book, but without the help of others, this book would not have been possible. I'd like to thank everyone that helped create this book.

Firstly to my goats - this book would not have been possible without you and your milk.

Thank you to my lovely husband, for your taste testing, proofreading, patience, and sense of humour.

Thank you to all my children, for motivating and encouraging me in cheesemaking, asking questions, helping, and taste testing,

Thanks to everyone that gave nice feedback about my cheeses.

Thank you to the community at Permies.com for providing helpful feedback, encouragement, community, and a friendly place to share stuff. You all deserve bacon, cheese, sparkles, and pie.

Thank you to the beta-reading team, in particular Leigh at 5 Acres and a Dream, Penelope Blackmer, and Paul Fookes. Whether you picked up on awkward errors, suggested things I could add in or improve, or gave encouragement when I was on the right track, your help made this book far better than I could have alone - thank you!

Thank you to everyone that backed this on Kickstarter and helped make the printing of this book possible, including Margaret Birtley AM, Brian Hanford 3H.R. Homestead, T. Rooney, Paulie, Better with Thyme Farm, Bigmech, Give Me Faith Farm, Bill Erickson eats breakfast with Spiderman, Matthew "Just plant more trees" Johnson, mahBarker, Olivia Ross, Marnix, Aimee Eliason, Stéphane Pothin, Trevar Moore, Pascal, Ozzie & Charlotte Nissen, Sophie Lacson-Lambinet Composer for Hire, Longboat Smoker, Gosia, David, Birgit Musil-Schläffer, Katya Sethi, Pete Jenney, Rick, Megan Scrivens, Daniël Kersing, Blake J. Riley, Jason Gray, Adam Szmyt from Poland, Douglas Rochler, Paul Tipper and Deb Montague at the farm on Rombo Hill NSW, Mark Payton, Pam H, Lisa Pimental, Crazy Plant Lady Wendy O'Neill, Alisha "the cheesiest love" Hill, Joe & Kate Van Meter, Jacobus Remmers Fonkel One, Percherider, Cosmic Hammer, Marcia Burgmann, Christina F., Barry C, Donna Mac Rae, Echo Mae, Eva, Susan Barr, Heidi Soldridge, Hunter C., Josh, Bethanee & Travis Wright, Josh Scheibe, Julian Kelly, Catalina Rodriguez Castañeda, Mikel Stous, Daniel Andres and W.E.B. Permaculture. Thank you all!

Thanks to everyone that helped with the Kickstarter in many ways, including Paul Wheaton, Carla Burke, Joylynn Hardesty, Beau M. Davidson, Mike Haasl, Ashley at Practical Self Reliance, the Permaculture Research Institute, Grass Roots magazine, Hobby Farms magazine, Adam J Klaus, Raven Ranson, Thomas J Elpel, and Leigh Tate.

Contents

Introduction..................................6
My cheesemaking journey. Cheesemaking and survival. About small batch cheesemaking.

The Ingredients of Cheesemaking..........11
Milk: Choosing, storing, handling, seasonality, producing at home.
Rennet: Choosing, diluting, testing, making and working with homemade rennets.
Homemade cultures.
Salt.

Cheesemaking Equipment...................32
Basic cheesemaking equipment.
Advanced cheesemaking equipment.
Ways to press cheeses.
How to use gentle heat during the cheesemaking process.

Learning to Make Cheese, Step by Step...38
Finding cheeses that work for you.

Understanding Cheesemaking...............42
Cheesemaking in detail: cutting curds, stirring, optional steps, shaping, pressing, salting, and more.

Aging Cheeses.............................59
Creating your own cheese aging space, working with moulds, different methods of aging.

How to use Leftover Whey.................68
In the kitchen, in the garden, on the homestead.

Cheese Recipes............................71
Ricotta and paneer..............................72
Yoghurt cheese..................................74
Farmers cheese and quark........................75
A spotlight on chèvre and other slow-cultured cheeses...77
Easy chèvre, soft cheese, or cream cheese.......78
The many ways of aging chèvre...................81
    Crottin....................................81
    Air-dried chèvre...........................82
    Aged chèvre with a herbed or spiced rind..82
    Ladled curd aged chèvre....................82

Leaf-wrapped chèvre..........................83
Chèvre in oil................................83
Fast mozzarella..............................84
Slow cultured mozzarella.....................86
Focusing on feta and other brined cheeses....88
Feta...90
Halloumi.....................................92
Tomme..94
The washed curd technique....................96
Havarti and Gouda............................98
All about Alpine cheese.....................100
Gruyère and Emmental........................102
Bloomy white rind cheeses...................104
Optimum bloomy rind aging process...........105
Camembert and Brie..........................106
Simplified jar-cultured Camembert...........108
Blue cheeses................................110
Cheddar.....................................112
Traditional Cheddar and Caerphilly..........114
Parmesan-style grating cheese...............116
Whey ricotta................................117
Norwegian Whey Cheese (Gjetost).............118

Other Dairy Products....................120
Kefir.......................................120
Yoghurt.....................................120
    Viili and room temperature yoghurt.....121
    Greek and Bulgarian yoghurt............122
Sour cream and cultured butter..............123
Ghee (clarified butter).....................124
Custard.....................................124
No-Churn Ice Cream..........................125

Appendix A: Troubleshooting.............126
Cheesemaking troubleshooting................126
Aging troubleshooting.......................131
Appendix B: Hard cheese quick reference.134
Appendix C: Rennet and culture doses....135
Appendix D: Cheese diary example........136
Index.......................................138

Introduction

A peasant approach to cheesemaking

The word peasant originally meant "country dweller". It could be defined as self-sufficiency, homesteading, and producing food at a small scale. The modern dictionary has redefined it into something completely different, but I like to reclaim the old version of the word, which has to do with the land and rural life.

A peasant approach to cheesemaking involves working with seasonal conditions, small amounts of land, and busy varied lives, to produce food. The peasant was not concerned if she was making a cheese that the city people would call "artisan", she just got on with the job, preserved the milk in the form of cheese, and that is how all the fantastic cheeses we now know came about: not in labs and industrial farms, but in home kitchens, using the milk from the home dairy herd that was milked by hand.

Peasant cheesemaking was usually the work of the woman of the house. She had many tasks beyond cheesemaking, and developed cheeses that would complement this way of life. Recipes and traditions were passed down through generations, reflecting the best kinds of cheeses to be made within the conditions of a particular region. Wooden cheesemaking tools were also passed down, their porous surfaces filled with beneficial cultures from many generations of raw milk cheesemaking, giving even more unique tastes to the cheeses. We can reclaim this word and this tradition, passing on our prized natural cultures and locally adapted recipes to future generations.

My Cheesemaking Journey

I've always been interested in making things from scratch, and learning how things used to be done before the age of supermarkets. Cheesemaking was always part of the long-term plan of getting dairy animals, but my main motivation was the fresh raw milk to feed to my family.

My first summer with goats, I found new homes for the goat kids once they were old enough to be weaned and was faced with an abundance of milk. I didn't mind milking twice a day - at that time in my life I found it to be a settling influence. There was something nourishing about spending time with goats, and not just the milk they gave us - it was a relationship of give and take: they needed us, and we needed them, and twice a day, every day, I would walk them up to the milking stand and sit down milking, half concentrating on the milking, half staring off at the farmlands beyond, knowing I would be milking them from somewhere different soon, and that it didn't matter where it was so much, but that they would be there, providing us with milk and goatness in our lives.

I got some cheesemaking books from the library. Some I liked more than others. I got all the gear I thought I needed to have to get started, and a bunch of cultures, packed in plastic.

I followed the recipes, step by step, and had mostly good results. I experimented with aging cheeses in different places in rental houses without any electricity.

After a while of making my own cheeses, I began to question the recipes and read between the lines. One book I had was talking about traditional cheesemaking in France and it sounded like a very simple process that would be illegal in this country, but it worked there, and had worked for a long time.

I diluted the citric acid with water for mozzarella and wondered "could I just use vinegar instead?"

For other cheeses, I began to wonder - "do I need to do all of this exactly as the recipe says?"

Do I really need to stand here for 45 minutes stirring constantly?

How were things done in earlier times?

Gradually I began to experiment. First it was using cider vinegar instead of diluted citric acid in mozzarella - it worked - and I'd replaced one plastic packet with local ingredients.

I started making my chèvre with homemade kefir instead of powdered cultures, and it turned out just as good. Another plastic packet was gone, and replaced with local ingredients.

Gradually I gained the confidence to follow instincts, try more stuff, and just take the cheesemaking process back to the absolute basics. At the end of the day, we are turning milk into a solid food. There are many ways to do this - some of them are quick and need to be used within a few days, others are done to preserve the summer milk for the winter months. At the end of the day, if we are achieving our aim, and it works, it doesn't matter so much if we follow a recipe exactly, or if we can call it this cheese name or that - most of the cheeses we know of are named after a particular place, and they are essentially an expression of terroir and ancestral tradition, not a recipe from a book.

At some point I wanted to teach this simplicity to others - to inspire them to create their first ricotta from stuff they already had at home and turn it into a meal. I figured out the way I would want this all taught to me and started teaching.

And after many years making cheeses I feel that my style of cheesemaking needs a book of its own. Now I present my recipes to you, along with more information about making cheese from a homesteader's perspective, to begin your cheesemaking journey, and to inspire you to think outside the box and create cheeses that truly reflect your local surroundings.

About this book

My aim with this book is to provide recipes for many cheeses, along with the background information to be able to succeed in many different circumstances, make your own varieties of cheese, and also to troubleshoot when things are not perfect. To keep the recipes uncluttered and easy to reference, I've tried to find a balance between explaining the processes earlier in the book and keeping the recipes simple to minimise page-turning.

If you've never made a cheese before and are eager to dive in right away, the ricotta and paneer recipes can be followed as-is. For cultured and rennetted cheeses, I encourage you to first read the sections on culture and rennet in the "Understanding the cheesemaking process" section on pages 42 to 58, so that you will understand how culture and rennet are added, what a clean break looks like, and when to cut the curds. Also in this section are the descriptions of the other steps you will encounter in cheesemaking, such as cutting curds, stirring, draining, pressing, and other steps that create unique cheeses. This part of the book also covers the aging process and different options for cheese rinds.

The earliest pages of this book on cheesemaking ingredients and equipment go into detail about milk, cultures, rennet, equipment, and other elements of cheesemaking. These are for people who want a deep understanding of how different choices impact the finished cheese. The first of these pages is called "It all starts with milk", as the impact of milk choice upon cheesemaking really cannot be overstated. If you follow the book from cover to cover, you'll learn how each ingredient that goes into the cheese affects the final cheese, followed by the processes, and finally the recipes, where all the knowledge is put into practise to make great cheeses.

Once you have made a few cheeses, a lot of the descriptive steps don't really need to be read, which is why I've created the quick reference guide with each recipe where possible – you can just quickly glance at the page and know when each step needs to be done, what temperature needs to be reached, what size to cut the curds, and so on.

Why small batch cheesemaking?

On a small homestead scale it can be tricky to get enough fresh milk at once to make a standard 20 litre (5 gallon) batch of homemade cheese. Even a 2 gallon (eight litre) size batch found in several books is out of reach for many cheesemakers. For people wanting to learn this skill without their own animals, having to experiment with such huge amounts of milk puts an expensive barrier in front of what can be a really rewarding process.

The fresher the milk used in the cheese, the better the cheese will be, so for anyone with a small amount of milk coming in each day, it can make sense to use all of that milk at once for a small batch cheese rather than saving it up over several days for a larger batch.

Small batch hard cheeses take less time to age, so there's less time to wait before eating.

With small batches, there is more scope for experimentation - you can experiment with different variations, adding spices and herbs to cheeses, finishing rinds in different ways, and creating your own cheeses, without worrying about ruining a huge batch of cheese.

Less time is needed to eat a whole cheese: When opening a huge wheel of cheese it all needs to be eaten before it starts going bad. Small cheeses can stay whole, and if you open one up, it can be used fairly quickly and will not go bad, even if you don't have a fridge. You can just leave an opened small cheese with a wedge taken out of it in the cheese cave without needing to fuss about wrapping it up, refrigerating it, or having exact plans for how to use it.

Making cheeses smaller and more frequently means there is less of a "my precious" attitude about opening a cheese - you don't have to wait for a special occasion - it can be something that happens quite often, it could even be a part of your life every week.

How small is a small batch? How can I scale down a recipe?

If you have only a quart or litre or two of milk, you can make chèvre, aged chèvre, Camembert, ricotta, paneer, or even a small batch of mozzarella, feta, or halloumi.

If you have a gallon (four litres), you can make some hard cheeses such as Havarti and Gouda, if your gallon of milk is high in solids (such as it is in winter or later in the lactation curve), you can make any of the cheeses in this book.

If you have five or six quarts (five or six litres), you can make any hard cheese.

If you have two gallons (eight litres), you can make any hard cheese, and the rennet may be easier to measure.

The type of milk you're using will impact the cheese that you're making – thin summer milk or milk from animals that give less protein will produce less cheese than thick winter milk or milk from animals that give higher amounts of protein and fat in the milk. Observe your cheese yields through the seasons, and you may find that you can make a good hard cheese from three litres (or quarts) of thick winter milk.

Why natural cheesemaking?

Some people like to buy a packet of this, a can of that, and mix it together. Other people like to make things entirely from scratch, from ingredients we can find in nature, fermented with cultures that we can perpetuate at home. I am one of the latter people.

Making cheese with natural cultures brings more variation into the process. We never know exactly which aspects of the culture are going to be flourishing in the cheese today. Different subtleties of temperature, storage conditions, length of culturing and much more can impact the taste of a cheese. Every cheese I've made this way has been delicious in its own way, like a real meal from scratch is. I get great satisfaction in working with resilient homemade cultures rather than a packet of something, and I hope this book will inspire you to do the same.

A natural approach to cheesemaking reflects the traditional cheeses of the past, where instead of relying on purchased packets of particular cultures and moulds, the natural surroundings and flora are respected, and different cheeses are the specialties of different areas.

The natural approach to cheesemaking is perfect for homesteading and self reliance.

Cheesemaking and survival

Cheese was once made for survival: taking a highly perishable liquid and turning it into a solid food. Some of these cheeses would be used shortly, as a nourishing staple food, others would last through the cold dark winters, providing food while the local dairy animals are dry. The specialties of different regions developed as different approaches towards these aims, working with the natural conditions of the area, finding the most suitable ways of transforming milk for them.

Just as the different regions of the past developed their own specialities, we can develop our own specialities suited to our own local conditions. My homestead focuses on several cheeses: the chèvre family of slowly coagulated lactic curd cheeses, for the mostly hands-off transformation of milk into lactic curd cheeses that are used fresh, frozen, or aged into dried rind and bloomy rind cheese; everyday cooking cheeses, such as mozzarella and paneer, for making a simple staple food during cheesemaking season (or freezing it for the off-season); washed curd cheese such as Havarti, as we love the mild milky taste, pliable texture, and short aging time; tomme, for its simplicity, taste, and adaptability; cooked curd cheeses, such as Emmental, for their long-keeping qualities and delightful slightly caramelised taste. I also make a lot of gjetost, which takes what is sometimes seen as a waste product (whey) and transforms it with the help of our woodstove into a delicious spread packed full of B vitamins and other goodness. There are many more cheeses that I'll make every now and then, but these are what I focus on when providing food for my family.

I think sometimes it helps to go back to basics and focus on the survival aspect of cheesemaking.

The beginning of a great cheese: it all starts with milk.

The Ingredients of Cheesemaking

It all starts with milk...

If you leave a jar of raw milk sitting at a warm room temperature, it will turn into cheese on its own. Most people prefer the taste of rennetted cheeses, but to watch a jar of milk transform into curds and whey, and then to strain it, can be a good learning experience – milk wants to transform into cheese on its own.

Cheese is a complicated subject, with the basics obscured sometimes by the overwhelming amount of different traditions that grew on their own, in many isolated places. Some cheeses have names that can't legally be used outside a locality - to protect the integrity of the cheeses that can be produced only by animals eating the plants that grow in particular locations, or the aging conditions in a particular cave.

In writing this book I aim to shed light on a continuous thread that runs through all these traditions - respect for the animals and their milk, the natural processes involved, and of working with nature to produce the kinds of cheeses that work best in a particular area. Bloomy white rind cheeses are the specialty of the regions around Brie and Camembert because the milk produced by the animals there has the perfect bacteria, and the aging conditions are right for developing these rinds. In the past, when I fed my goats mostly on lucerne while surrounded by cattle farms, I wasn't able to develop the white rinds, yet where I live now in the forest these rinds develop on their own, and my larder now filled not just with beautiful cheeses, but with traditional chorizo and salami as well.

In this book I present recipes that work to create familiar styles of cheeses. Many people won't be inspired to try a cheese with an unfamiliar name or description, but when cheeses are described in terms of Gouda, Camembert, Gruyere, Stilton, feta, Cheddar, and so on, we can easily decide whether we're likely to enjoy the cheese or not. My hope with this book is to further develop cheesemaking tradition, so that homestead cheesemakers can come up with even more varieties of cheeses, while appreciating the traditional styles of cheese.

In some ways I wish to demystify the cheesemaking process, so that anyone can do it; in other ways, I wish to develop even more mystery in the development of home cheesemaking processes - I want to encourage you to be creative, to come up with new varieties, to follow instincts in creating new flavours, new processes, new aging techniques that work with your homestead.

This book is not just for homesteads. I write it for anyone who loves cheese, and wants to try making their own. Some care is required in the selection of milk. Raw milk from healthy animals fed a natural diet is always the best choice, but if you can't access raw milk, there are other choices that will work.

Animals fed silage or lots of grain will make milk that reacts differently in cheesemaking to the milk from grass-fed or forested animals. Small amounts of grain are often fed to animals as a treat at milking time, and this doesn't affect cheesemaking, but large amounts of grain fed as a staple source of calories will often cause an animal health problems and make their milk less suitable for cheesemaking.

Hay is often fed to animals during winter or drought, and cheese can be made from the milk of hay-fed animals, although it often doesn't end up having quite as much flavour or nutrition as cheese made from animals eating fresh plants.

Here is an explanation of which milks will and won't work for cheese:

Raw milk: The best

Raw milk from healthy animals fed a natural diet is milk as it's intended to be. Raw milk contains many intricacies that add to the flavour of the cheese, especially during aging.

It's always best to know the source of raw milk, to make sure that the animals are healthy, as some livestock diseases can be transmitted to people from milk.

Accessing raw milk

The most rewarding way for accessing raw milk is to keep dairy animals yourself. This is why I wrote *Backyard Dairy Goats*, because it is possible, even in suburban rental yards.

Raw milk can sometimes be found as "pet milk" or "bath milk", with "not suitable for human consumption" written on the bottle. Packaged dog food also has this warning, and I don't know of any dog food companies getting sued because someone thought it was a good idea to eat it, but it is a legally weird area in my country to sell raw milk as pet milk, so I won't suggest making cheese from this milk in case I end up in legal trouble.

In some places farmers are being forced to add nasty-tasting stuff to their bath milk to stop people from drinking it, so it's best to check this first! Again, it is a weird legal area, so I won't suggest making cheese from "bath milk" either, in case someone tries to get me in legal trouble.

Herdshare is a type of CSA (Community Supported Agriculture) where you can sign up to own part of a farmer's herd, and because it is legally your herd now, you can drink the milk without the nanny-state declaring an emergency. Herdshares can be as small as one homesteader offering a few people a share of their one or two cows, for example, seven people could share one cow, each of them milking (or receiving the milk) from the cow one day per week. Herdshares can be larger in scale and more organised as well, with some of them designed to provide their herdshare communities with milk all through the year.

Approaching dairy farmers directly is possible, and to help them with legal issues you could say that you want raw milk to feed orphaned kittens or bobby calves. If they find out you are buying it to drink, they may not sell it to you so that they don't get in trouble with the law.

In some states and countries, access to raw milk is more simple than this, and it can be found in shops, in vending machines, and directly from farms and homesteads. For more information about legal access to raw milk, see www.realmilk.com

Storing and handling raw milk for cheesemaking

Raw milk without anything contaminating it actually keeps better than pasteurised milk. A jar of raw milk, filled close to the top and not opened will keep for quite a while, and if it is good, uncontaminated milk, it will start to sour on its own, and will just taste like soured milk - sometimes a pleasant drink.

Once a jar has been opened, whether it be raw or pasteurised, yeasts and bacteria floating in the air have a chance to get into the jar. Generally the lower the level of milk is in the jar, the quicker it will spoil. I am mindful about this when making raw cheeses, only using older jars of milk if they haven't been opened. Opened jars are fine for ricotta and paneer.

Raw cheeses are best made when the milk is fairly fresh. Fresh milk gives less chance for unwanted bacteria to grow, and as milk ages, the protein structures begin to change, giving you a lower cheese yield.

When I had a fridge, I would try to make cheese within 3 days of milking, and if I had older milk I would turn it into paneer, ricotta, and mozzarella. Without a fridge, the amount of time milk will last depends on how I am storing it, and what the weather is like. If I am storing it immersed in a river or surrounded by ice bricks, it will last as long as it would in the fridge. If I am just relying on our not-perfect larder, it will start to sour much more quickly, and 24 hours after milking it has sometimes already turned to curds and whey on the hottest summer days, and all that needs to be done is to strain it to use as a soft farmers cheese. If I wanted to make any cultured or rennetted cheeses on days like this, I would need to start them shortly after milking.

One of my strategies these days, now that I milk once a day and get between four and eight litres of milk every morning during the peak season, is to use all the milk from one morning for raw cheesemaking, while using the stored milk from the previous day for drinking, yoghurt, and cooking.

When using the very freshest milk, cheese yields are higher, the acidifying process more predictable, and there's less chance of unwanted bacteria getting a chance to multiply. This strategy will also work for someone with one house cow, or for anyone that brings home fresh milk from a farmer. In general, the sooner after milking that you can start your cheesemaking, the better your cheese will be (although for best results wait for at least two hours after milking to begin cheesemaking, as raw milk contains an antibacterial substance that disappears after two hours).

Non-homogenised milk: Second place

Pasteurised but not homogenised milk (also called "cream top") is becoming increasingly available, and can be a good choice if you can't access raw milk. Pasteurised goats milk has usually not gone through the homogenisation process, but the fat globules are much smaller than those in cows milk, so although it appears to look like homogenised milk, it can be treated as non-homogenised milk and used for all kinds of cheesemaking.

As with raw milk, using the freshest milk possible will give better cheese yields, so if you are buying your milk from a shop, try to find out which day the milk is delivered, and for best results get your cheesemaking milk soon after that.

Homogenised milk: Only suitable for some cheeses, or with calcium chloride

Pasteurised *and* homogenised milk is the standard supermarket milk in my country, and in many others. Milk is put under high pressure and forced through small holes to break up the fat globules.

This is done for cosmetic reasons and increased shelf life, and it is a fairly new process, so it's hard to say what the long-term health effects are.

The homogenisation also breaks up the proteins into smaller pieces, and for hard cheeses the curd needs these proteins in their whole form in order to set properly, so making cheese with homogenised milk is unreliable for hard cheeses, but can be used successfully for ricotta, paneer, mozzarella, and soft cheeses.

Calcium chloride is usually added to hard cheeses made from homogenised milk, in order to get the curds to set properly. This is a packaged additive that I personally avoid, but if your only option for making cheese is homogenised milk and you desperately want to make hard cheeses, it might be worth looking into, just be very careful with the dose, as too much calcium chloride can cause a bitter taste in the cheese.

Different packages of calcium chloride will have different dosage instructions, so look at the packet and very carefully measure out the exact amount to use. Calcium chloride is stirred into the milk five minutes before adding the rennet.

Ultra-pasteurised (UHT) milk: avoid this!

Ultra-pasteurised and UHT milk are homogenised milks that are heated to above 116°C (240°F). Heating to such high temperatures alters the milk structure so much that these milks will not work at all for cultured and rennetted cheeses. They will work for yoghurt, ricotta, and paneer, but the cheese yields will be lower and the texture and taste not as good. The long-term health effects of this high temperature treatment have also not been studied.

These milks were first only found as shelf-stable milks, but increasingly more milk in supermarket fridges has been ultra-pasteurised, so if you are using supermarket milk, make sure to check the label.

Goat milk, cow milk, sheep milk, buffalo milk?

All milks behave differently in cheesemaking. Milk from individual animals within a herd will vary, and even the milk of an animal will vary throughout the seasons, with richer milk at the start of lactation and in the colder months, and milk with less solids in the summer. In general, cows milk is the most commonly used for cheesemaking, the beta carotene in cows milk leaves a familiar yellowy colour in the cheese.

Goats convert beta carotene into retinol (true vitamin A) more efficiently than cows, so their milk is pure white in colour, and the cheeses made from it are white. The different colour can take some getting used to for people only used to cows cheeses. Raw goats milk can give a different depth of flavour to cheeses. The taste of a goats cheese will change depending on what the goat is eating - goats on pasture or hay create milder cheeses, whereas goats browsing in the forest and on scrub can create more interesting flavours. All goats cheese that I've eaten has been great, whether my goats have been living in my backyard and fed on lucerne, or free ranging in the forest.

The cheese yield from goats milk is usually slightly less than for cows milk. The curds from goats milk are sometimes softer, an advantage for chèvre and other soft cheeses, but more care sometimes need to be taken when making hard cheese from goats milk.

Sheeps milk is very dense. It has its own delicious flavour, and like goats milk, is purely white. Sheeps milk will make more cheese per litre used than cows milk, so you can use one gallon (four litres) of sheeps milk to follow a 6 litre (6 quart) cheese recipe by keeping all other ingredients the same and just using less milk to get the same yield.

Water buffalo milk is famously used in mozzarella, but can be used in any cheese recipe. Buffalo milk is also white, and the cheese yields are higher than for cows milk.

Organic milk or non organic? Certified or uncertified?

Certified organic milk has strict standards for antibiotic use and hormones, and organic certification is usually a good indicator that the milk won't contain any weird nasty stuff when you can't produce your own or buy directly from farmers.

Where I live, hormone implants for dairy animals are banned, but in the USA, these hormones are not banned, with their use only being prohibited in certified organic animals, so for health reasons it is worth seeking out milk from animals that don't have hormone implants, whether they are certified organic, or a local farm that you know and trust.

Fat to protein ratio

For typical cheesemaking, the ideal ratio of fat to protein in milk is 1:1. Most milks are fairly close to this ratio, but far higher ratios of fat can be found in Jersey cow milk and water buffalo milk. For hard cheeses made from Jersey milk, many cheesemakers partially skim the milk before cheesemaking, as the extra fat in the milk can have trouble staying in the curd during the stirring process. For some cheeses, the extra fat can be a positive thing, helping to create naturally creamy and rich soft cheeses, or the strong flavours in pecorino-style cheeses.

For the most part, the fat to protein ratio can be ignored, but Jersey cow owners may need to keep this in mind and either partially skim the milk, or be very gentle during the stirring process.

Milk and seasonality

Milk changes throughout the lactation cycle. Early in lactation, the milk is higher in lactose (milk sugar). Lactose provides food for the starter cultures, so milk with a higher amount of lactose will result in faster culturing. Later in the season, there's less lactose, so culturing can be slower. Taking notes and observing your cheesemaking through the year will help you to determine whether to add more culture at certain times of year, whether to allow more or less time for cheeses to culture, and the results you can expect during the seasons.

The fat and protein content of milk also changes through the seasons. Early in lactation, there are high amounts of both protein and fat, and it's often easy to make great chèvre. As the lactation progresses, the milk can be quite watery, and cheese yields can be low because of this. Cheeses made at this time, if you follow the standard doses of rennet, can end up behaving more like Parmesan-style cheeses which are made from skimmed milk with higher doses of rennet. At this time of year I often give up on making chèvre for a while, as it's very difficult to get nice soft cheese curds that aren't dry or rubbery. On the other hand, this stage of lactation is perfect for making many hard cheeses – eye-forming bacteria thrive in lower fat milk (some mountain cheeses are made from partially skimmed milk in order to encourage this), and very hard cheeses for grating over pasta seem to just make themselves.

Often the later stages of lactation coincide with autumn and winter. During this time, the protein and fat content increase, making for a milk with high amounts of solids, and it's possible to easily make great chèvre again. Hard cheeses made during this time end up with higher cheese yields, so it's possible to get a decent sized small batch hard cheese with just three or four litres or quarts of milk.

If you're making cheese at a time of year when the milk is low in solids, consider reducing the rennet dose (or keep it the same, if you want your cheese to be a very hard cheese). If you're making cheese at a time of year with high amounts of solids, increase the rennet dose, or reduce the amount of milk used in the whole recipe, for example, in summer I might use eight litres (2 gallons) of milk to make a hard cheese, with the same amount of rennet and culture that I'd use for making the same cheese in winter using four litres (1 gallon) of milk.

Storing milk for cheesemaking

In French goat cheesemaking tradition, raw milk that is to be used within 48 hours is not cooled any lower than 10°C (50°F). Lower temperatures than this make for slower coagulation, and the growth of unwanted bacteria in very clean raw milk is not much higher at 10°C than at fridge temperatures.

Pasteurised milk will need to be kept as cold as possible, in low fridge temperatures of 5°C (40°F) or lower.

As milk ages, no matter how cold it is stored, the proteins begin to change so that you'll end up with more protein in the whey and less in the curd, making less cheese. To slow down the aging process of the milk if you are storing it longer than 48 hours, it can be carefully frozen.

To freeze milk, place in jars, preferably wide-mouth ones, and leave at least an inch of space at the top of the jar (or two inches or more if it angles sharply at the top) to allow for the milk to expand during the freezing process. Keep them upright in the freezer to avoid leaking.

Frozen jars are very brittle, so be gentle when moving them around.

To defrost, just remove them from the freezer a few hours before you make cheese and keep at room temperature (or put them in the fridge overnight).

If you don't want to freeze milk and need to keep your milk for longer than two days, try to keep the milk as cold as possible. The fridge door is the worst spot of all for milk, as the temperature is constantly changing, and it is often warmer than the rest of the fridge. Storing milk on the top shelf of the fridge, towards the back will help it keep for longer. Avoid putting hot jars of leftovers in the fridge, and avoid putting large containers of anything at room temperature right next to the jars. For the best storage of milk in a fridge, keep the temperature as close to 1°C (34°F) as possible.

If you might be drinking some of the stored milk, it's better to decant it into smaller jars, and store the cheesemaking milk in a full jar at the back of the fridge, and have a separate jar for drinking, as removing a jar of milk from the fridge will warm it up slightly, and having part of the jar open to oxygen, and opening the lid to get drinks from it give more opportunity for unwanted things to get into the milk.

Sometimes unhelpful bacteria can multiply in the milk during storage and create a curd with gassy bubbles (see the troubleshooting appendix at the end of this book for more about this). If you're concerned about this happening, you can pasteurise the stored milk right before cheesemaking by heating it to 63°C (145°F) and holding it at that temperature for 30 minutes. If you have fresh raw milk available, this can be added to the cheese pot after the stored milk has finished pasteurising, bringing some of the benefits of raw milk to the cheese.

Understanding culture and bacteria growth in milk

Bacteria growth in milk depends on four factors:
- The type of bacteria present.
- How much of it there is.
- The temperature it is stored at.
- The time it is stored for.

Different types of bacteria multiply at different rates, favouring different temperature ranges, and having different effects on the cheese. Coliforms are the main nemesis of the cheesemaker, as these multiply rapidly and ruin cheeses. Slowly cultured cheeses, such as chèvre, even if made from very fresh milk that is contaminated with enough coliforms will often have gassy bubbles and nasty flavours. If you are having trouble with coliform contamination, it is best to look at your source of milk and the milk handling practises (see the next section for more on this), or to focus on hard cheeses and other fast-cultured cheeses.

The amount of bacteria present plays a role: A small amount of contamination in the milk, if the milk is used fast enough, will soon be eclipsed by the hefty dose of good bacteria in the kefir or other starter culture. If the contamination is very bad, then the unwanted bacteria may be enough to ruin your cheese even with the addition of starter cultures.

Bacteria, both wanted and unwanted types, grows much faster at 20°C (68°F) and above than at lower temperatures. At 10°C (50°F) and below, growth is much slower.

Time plays an equally important role in bacteria growth. For the first two hours after milking, milk contains an anti-bacterial substance that prevents both wanted and unwanted bacteria from growing. If culture is added shortly after milking, after these two hours are over it quickly begin to acidify the milk and fills the niches that unwanted bacteria would otherwise colonise. The longer the milk is allowed to sit beyond that first two hours, the more time the unwanted bacteria has to multiply.

How all of this works in practise, on my homestead, is that I first aim to produce very clean milk from very healthy animals, using very clean equipment. If I am making chèvre or other slow-cultured cheeses, I aim to get them started very early in the day, to give the kefir culture a chance to rapidly colonise the milk before anything else can. If I am making hard cheese and other fast cultured cheeses, I often leave it until later in the day, storing the milk in a cooler place, somewhere between 10°C (50°F) and 15°C (59°F) is great if I can find it. If it is a very hot day, and I can't find anywhere below 20°C (68°F) to keep the milk, I either start my hard cheeses quite early in the day, put the milk in the freezer, or if I haven't gotten around to making the cheese and it's getting late, I will use it to make paneer, ricotta, or quick mozzarella.

So from the above, you can see that I am first reducing the **number** of unwanted bacteria and discouraging the bad **types** of bacteria with clean milking practises from healthy animals, I am then observing the **temperature** for bacteria growth and **timing** my cheesemaking based on the temperature and the type of cheese.

Different cheesemakers and homesteaders will find approaches that will work for them, but if you keep in mind those four factors, you can adapt your own cheesemaking to work with your local conditions.

Growing your own milk

Raising dairy animals can be a complicated subject, there are entire books dedicated to raising cows and goats, and I'd recommend reading one of these if you are serious about raising your own dairy animals.

While I can't go into the full joy and details of raising your own dairy animals here (I wrote *Backyard Dairy Goats* for that!), what I will share in this book are the optimum hygiene practises for harvesting and handling home-produced raw milk.

These are my suggestions for harvesting the cleanest possible milk for cheesemaking from a home dairy herd. This level of detail may make a beginner's head spin and is not always necessary (in fact, many traditional cheesemaking practises of the past involved using equipment that wasn't sterile but instead contained enough helpful bacteria to aggressively colonise the milk before nasties could get a foothold), but if you have been getting coliform contamination (gassy bubbles) in your cheeses, or if you just want to be certain that you are doing everything possible to avoid contaminating your cheeses with nasty stuff, these are my recommendations of practises to follow for the best possible milk:

- All animals are healthy and eating a natural diet. Some grain is fine, but not huge amounts. Don't use milk from animals with mastitis, antibiotic residue, or who appear to not be in full health.
- Don't feed silage.
- Avoid feeding anything from the cabbage family 3 hours or less before milking time. Use garlic only in small amounts, too much will change the taste of milk.
- Try to milk as regularly as possible – milk that has been left in the udder for too long can develop off-flavours and behave unpredictably in cheesemaking.
- Stainless steel is used for the milking bucket and funnel, glass is used for the jars.
- All equipment that will touch the milk is clean and heat-sterilised.
- Udders are clean and dry before milking. Goats udders can usually be brushed off with the back of the hand, cows udders often need to be washed with a warm wet towel, and thoroughly dried.
- For even cleaner milk, use a nut milk bag or a large piece of cheesecloth over the top of the milking bucket while milking, to first pre-strain the milk as it comes out of the udder.
- Straight after milking, the milk is quickly strained through cheesecloth into the jars.
- If cheese is to be made the same day of milking, it begins roughly two hours after milking, or the milk is cooled quickly to 10°C (50°F). If milk is to be kept for longer than two days it is best if it's chilled to below 5°C (40°F), ideally 1°C (34°F).
- Kefir or yoghurt to be used for a starter culture is freshly fed from milk produced with the above standards. Whey as a starter culture is fresh and from a good batch of cheese.

How to heat-sterilise milking equipment

Wash everything first with lukewarm water, to remove traces of milk, animal hair, and anything else. Having water on your jars will also help them not to crack when they come into contact with boiling water.

Boil water, and take it off the heat, so that it is still scalding hot, but is no longer actively bubbling. Put your glass jars on a dry wooden surface or a dry towel, and carefully pour a small amount of boiled water into each jar, shake it around the jar and the lid, then pour out. Add a larger amount of boiled water to the jar and shake again, to completely coat all surfaces of the jar and lid with the scalding water to sterilise them.

Put the funnel and cheesecloth in the milking bucket. Pour boiling water all over the inside of the bucket, filling it up to above the level of the funnel and cheesecloth. Put the lid on and leave to sit until you're ready to begin milking. I leave mine overnight.

How to encourage helpful bacteria in non-sterile milking and cheesemaking gear

Salt rubbed onto surfaces will encourage helpful bacteria and funguses at the expense of unwanted bacteria, while also getting into pores and cracks and drying out the surfaces. Salt is ideal for rubbing onto wood. Non-raw vinegar such as cheap white cleaning vinegar is a good cleaning agent that brings acidity to various surfaces, discouraging unwanted bacteria and moulds.

The more traditional food production and preservation practises that are taken up in the home kitchen, the more interesting and often-helpful bacteria will be in the air and on your kitchen surfaces. Jars of sauerkraut opened at mealtimes release small amounts lactobacteria into the kitchen, charcuterie encouraged to grow white moulds spread these delicious moulds to cheeses in the larder, kombucha, kefir, and kvass bring even more diverse helpful bacteria into the kitchen, sourdough has both yeasts and bacteria and some of this might be floating in the air. I run a sourdough bakery from my home kitchen while also making several cheeses a week and have never had problems with yeasts taking over my cheeses.

As a precaution against contamination by all these different traditional foods, I keep my kombucha in one corner of the kitchen, wash and dry my hands well in between making bread and making cheese, but otherwise I suspect that all these cultures are filling my kitchen with many kinds of helpful bacteria.

Colonising your milk as quickly as possible with milk kefir or another natural culture will inoculate your milk with good bacteria, which will grow quickly and make the milk unsuitable for bad bacteria to grow.

All about rennet

Rennet is added to cheeses in varying amounts to make different types of curds. For the very soft cheeses such as chèvre, the tiniest amount of rennet is added and no stirring is done, for harder cheese, more rennet is used, and more steps are taken after the curd has set to encourage the curds to firm up and expel more whey. The process of rennetting is often referred to as coagulation. The goal of the rennet enzymes is to turn the acidified milk into curds, and the remaining steps of cheesemaking encourage varying amounts of whey to leave the curds.

Rennet is traditionally made from one of the stomachs of a young ruminant. A small amount of rennet can go a long way, so on a homestead scale it can make sense to butcher a very young animal once in a while, prepare the rennet, and have the rennet last for your cheesemaking adventures for years to come, in the case of calves, or for several months for kid or lamb rennet.

Most home cheesemakers don't make their own rennet, but purchase rennet in tablet, powder, or liquid form. I prefer tablets or powder when I can find them, as they are a simpler form that is more shelf-stable, and has a smaller list of ingredients, but liquid rennet is often easier to find. For people that make a lot of cheese, powdered rennet is better value than tablets, but can be trickier to measure for small batches - small batch cheesemakers will want to have a set of tiny measuring spoons measuring as low as 1/64 teaspoon when working with powdered rennet.

The amount of rennet to use in a recipe will vary depending on the result you want it to create, as well as the strength of the rennet - a very soft chèvre, for instance, uses a tiny dose that is almost impossible to measure unless you're making it with half a gallon (2 litres) of milk or more. Feta, Cheddar, Gouda, mozzarella, and most other cheeses use a standard amount of rennet, which is usually around a quarter of a tablet, 1/32 of a teaspoon of powder, or 0.8ml of liquid rennet for four or five litres (around a gallon) of milk. Very hard cheeses such as Parmesan use up to double the standard amount.

It is usually easier to measure liquid rennet for small batches using a syringe rather than a teaspoon. There is also a set of tiny measuring spoons that can be found online, the set that I have measures in 'dash', 'drop', 'pinch', and so on, and each of these corresponds to a specific measurement such as 1/64th of a teaspoon. Great cheeses can also be made without exact accuracy. The most important thing to remember about the rennet amount is that you really do not want to add too much rennet to a soft cheese – this will result in rubbery curds. If I am measuring rennet for soft cheese and have any doubt about whether I have poured too much, I will throw some of the diluted rennet away rather than adding it all to the cheese.

When I am making a hard cheese with five or six litres of milk, I will often think about the result I would like, and also about the cheese yields I have had recently. In summer the milk is more watery than other times of the year, and needs less rennet to set the smaller amount of solids, so I will use a quarter of a tablet for five or six litres of milk. Sometimes if I would prefer for a cheese to be harder, or if I know the milk is likely to have quite a big cheese yield, I will use half a tablet to create that cheese. Sometimes I will just measure out a quarter plus roughly an eighth of a tablet to set six litres of milk. The same reasoning can be applied with powdered and liquid rennet to use more or less depending on the cheese you are making and the seasonal conditions of the milk.

For tomme cheeses, where the 'correct' amount of rennet to use varies from recipe to recipe, and I find that using half a tablet for six litres creates a happy medium for these cheeses.

The standard amount of rennet can change, depending on the milk that you're using. When the milk is richer in early lactation and in winter, more rennet can be used, when the milk has less solids, less rennet can be used. The only way to find out the best amount is to experiment and take notes. To begin with, just feel free to use the amount recommended on the rennet packet and see how that works for you.

Different breeds of animals and individual animals will produce different results with rennet than other ones, for example, the fattier milk from a Jersey cow can handle more rennet than the watery milk from a Frisian cow. If you're not sure how much rennet to use for a particular batch of cheese, it's best to have a think about the results you'd like – if you'd prefer a softer cheese and suspect that the milk you're using is very rich, feel free to use the standard amount of rennet. Brie-style cheeses, for example, sometimes have added cream to increase the fat content, but the amount of rennet is not increased. Parmesan-style cheeses are sometimes made from skimmed milk, while the rennet amount stays the same (or is increased), to create a very hard cheese.

When you're opening a new packet of rennet, always observe what the standard amount to use is, as some rennets will say 'double strength' on the pack, and others will just say how much rennet is needed to set a certain amount of milk, which may be more or less than other rennets that you've used in the past.

If the amount of rennet to use isn't written on the packet, you can make test batches of cheese, carefully noting down how much rennet was used and how it behaved, and that way you can easily figure out the best amount to use.

Choosing rennet

Animal rennet available for purchase is almost always from calves, and is also known as "traditional rennet". This kind of rennet is minimally processed and contains both natural chymosin and pepsin, as well as some salt to preserve it. It is a natural product so the exact amounts vary from batch to batch, but usually chymosin will make up around 90% of the active enzymes and pepsin around 10%. Animal rennet is my first choice for rennet, but it can sometimes be difficult to find.

Junket rennet is a form of animal rennet with many additives; it can be found in some grocery shops but is not suitable for hard cheesemaking.

Microbial rennet is a good GMO-free option for vegetarians. This kind of rennet is widely available, and a certified organic version can be found. Microbial rennet has a reputation for causing bitter flavours during long aging, but is not something I have noticed, and other cheesemakers I have spoken to have not noticed this either.

Chymosin rennet, also known as "fermented chymosin" is sometimes confusingly referred to as "vegetarian rennet" and is produced by genetic engineering to mimic one of the enzymes in traditional animal rennet. If you are trying to avoid GMOs and only have vegetarian rennets to choose from, you may have to ask questions to find out whether the vegetarian rennet is the non-GMO microbial rennet or the GMO chymosin.

There are also vegetable coagulants available, such as thistle rennet, which I'll share my recipe for below. These are not suitable for aged cows milk cheeses but are fine for all soft cheeses, and for aged goat and sheep cheeses.

How to dilute rennet

Rennet needs to be diluted in water just before adding to the milk, to help it spread evenly through all the milk.

The most important thing to remember about diluting rennet, is not to dilute it until the last possible minute before using it. Rennet will become deactivated if it's left to sit in water for too long before adding to your cultured milk.

It's important to use water that is not chlorinated or chloraminated. If you're not sure if your water has anything that might contaminate the cheese, feel free to filter or boil it first (just make sure it's cooled to room temperature before using).

If your water is alkaline, you may want to first add a drop of non-raw vinegar such as white cleaning vinegar to your water to increase the acidity of the water before adding the rennet, as rennet does not like a p.H above 7.0.

If you're working with rennet tablets, first use a spoon or fork to crush it into a powder in your jar or ramekin. If you are using powder, just add that to the jar as you would for tablets. Start adding water and mix it thoroughly to dissolve the powder. For liquid rennet, add the water first, and then add the rennet, mixing it thoroughly with a fork.

The dilution rate for rennet is roughly 20 ml of water to 1 ml of rennet, or around 2 tablespoons of water to every ¼ teaspoon of liquid rennet. For small batches, I never measure, I just add more water than is needed and that works out fine.

How to test rennet

If you're not sure if your rennet is still useable, or if the milk you're working with is good for cheesemaking, it's possible to test a small amount first before diving in to make a cheese.

The swirly test

Mix 9ml (scant 2 teaspoons) cool water with 0.9ml liquid rennet or ¼ of a tablet. In a separate clear measuring cup or jar, warm 60ml (¼ cup) milk to 33°C (91°F). Swirl the milk jar around in your hand while pouring all the diluted rennet in, start timing the seconds as soon as you've poured in all the rennet, continuing to swirl around. When small flecks of curd start to appear at the edges of the jar, stop timing.

If if takes less than 20 seconds for flecks to appear, then your rennet is good to go. If it takes longer than 20 seconds, there may be something wrong with your rennet, or there may be an issue with your milk. You can repeat the test using a higher amount of rennet, to see if it is just that you need to use more rennet than the recommended dose, or if you suspect it is a milk issue, then you may want to add calcium chloride to your hard cheese, or to make a soft cheese, paneer, or mozzarella instead.

The clean break test

Another test is to take 1 cup (240ml) of milk warmed to 33°C (91°F), in a separate bowl dilute a standard dose of rennet (¼ teaspoon liquid or ¼ tablet) into 2 tablespoons of water, thoroughly mix into the milk and leave to sit for a few minutes. After around 6 minutes there should be a clean break if your rennet is good to go at the standard dose.

Homemade vegetable rennet

Vegetable rennets are more suited to soft cheese than hard cheese, and can often be slower to coagulate than animal rennets. They can be used to make beautiful aged cheeses by following the aged chèvre recipes on page 81, substituting the tiny amount of rennet in the chèvre recipe for a regular dose of homemade plant rennet according to the directions for each plant below.

Thistle flower rennet

Thistle stamens can easily be collected and dried when they appear, and either used right away, or dried. The rennet process itself needs to be started ahead of time, at least a couple of hours before you begin making your cheese, preferably overnight.

1. Collect the purple flower stamens from the common thistle – use only the purple parts, not any other colour. The easiest way to do this is to take out a pair of scissors and a small bowl and snip the purple stamens off into the bowl directly from the plants. You can either grind them up now for rennet, or gently dry them by leaving them on a flat tea towel in a place with some airflow. Once dry, store them in an airtight jar.

2. For every 1 litre (1 quart) of milk you'll be culturing, add around 2 teaspoons of thistle stamens to a mortar and pestle and grind them up.

3. Add 10ml (2 teaspoons) water for every 1 teaspoon of stamens that you started with. Grind a bit more with the mortar and pestle, then leave to steep for a few hours, or overnight.

4. Grind again, then pour the thistle water through cheesecloth into your cultured milk, straining out the powder to use only the murky brown water as rennet. Squeeze the cheesecloth to extract every last drop.

Thistle rennet is best used for goat and sheep cheeses, or for cows milk cheeses aged less than five weeks.

Nettle rennet

Two ounces (56g) of fresh nettle leaves can be used to set 1 quart (1 litre) of milk by putting them in a saucepan with ¼ cup water, simmering for 30 minutes, and then adding a pinch of salt. Strain through cheesecloth as you would for thistle rennet.

Lady's bedstraw rennet

Lady's bedstraw adds a yellow colour to cheeses as well as acting as a coagulant - to use, chop and lightly bruise a handful of stalks for every litre (quart) of milk, wrap them in a small square of wet cheesecloth, then infuse in warm milk until the milk curdles.

Fig sap rennet

Fig sap can be used as a coagulant - to use, snap a twig off a fig tree, remove the leaves, and gather the sap as it leaks out. Use 5 drops of sap for every 1 litre (1 quart) of milk.

Artichoke rennet

Collect the stamens and/or seeds of artichokes and cardoons. Pound in a mortar and pestle with a small amount of water, then strain and add at the rate of 1 teaspoon liquid to 1 litre (1 quart) milk.

Thistle seed rennet

The white undeveloped seeds at the base of the dying purple petals of the common thistle can be used, along with the seeds of blessed thistle and milk thistle. Use these seeds at the rate of half to one teaspoon seeds per four litres (1 gallon) milk. If using mature seeds, you may need to use more of them.

Homemade rennet from animals

Step 1:
The first step is to harvest the abomasum of a calf, kid, or lamb. This is the milk stomach, and for the best rennet for hard cheesemaking it's best to harvest when the animal is two weeks old or younger. Sometimes they die of natural causes when very young, and this is how I have harvested it.

To harvest, carefully make a slit in the belly, all the way from the bottom of the ribcage downwards. You should be able to gently take the digestive organs out, ending up with a mass of small intestine, with a large intestine connected to that on one side, and on the other side several small stomachs.

The abomasum is the bag attached to the very start of the small intestine, with the smaller roundish omasum coming off the other side, and then other stomachs beyond that.

When I have done this, I had the diagram on the opposite page on the table next to me, which helped me to see the shape of the abomasum, and the way it's attached on one side to the small intestine.

In baby goats it didn't look exactly like the diagram - removing it all in the way I did meant that the stomachs were all over the place and not neatly put together like in the diagram, so I found out the placement by looking at the small intestine and finding the stomach end of it.

The abomasum can easily be torn away from the small intestine, and to detach it from the omasum and the other stomachs, just find the narrow neck of the abomasum, where it meets the omasum, and then cut through it with a knife.

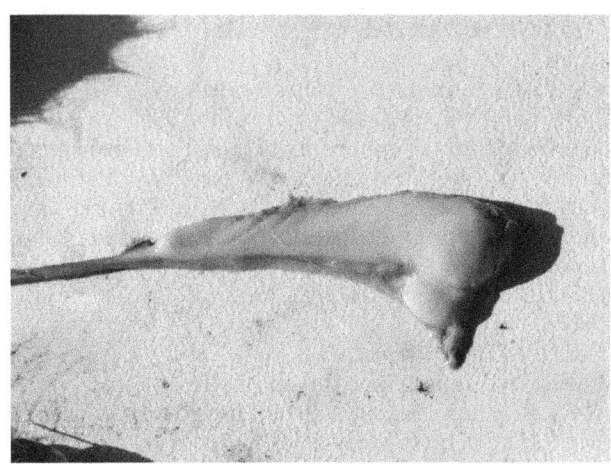
Goat abomasum, now detached and ready to process.

Step 2:
Gently rinse the abomasum under cold clean running water, turning it inside out and gently rinsing the inside until clean. The surface of the inside is wrinkly, and sometimes has curdled milk and other food in it.

Step 3:
Weigh the abomasum and place it in a glass container with a lid. Add 12 to 15% salt by weight (around 4 flat teaspoons of salt for every 100 grams of abomasum), and mix through just enough water to cover, then put the lid on and leave it to sit at around 20°C (68°F) for around 24-36 hours. Alternatively, you can dry-salt the abomasum by surrounding it completely with salt in a container and leaving it for two weeks.

Step 4: Remove the abomasum from the salt brine, and thread some cooking twine through it and hang it up to dry in a cool room (less than 20°C/68°F), preferably with good airflow, until it's hard and dry, which will take a week or two. If the humidity is too high where you live for air-drying, you can carefully dehydrate the salted abomasum instead in a food dehydrator, making sure the temperature stays below 40°C (104°F).

Step 5: Cut the dried salted abomasum into small pieces, and store in an airtight container.

Salted and dried abomasum hanging in between the garlic and the mead.

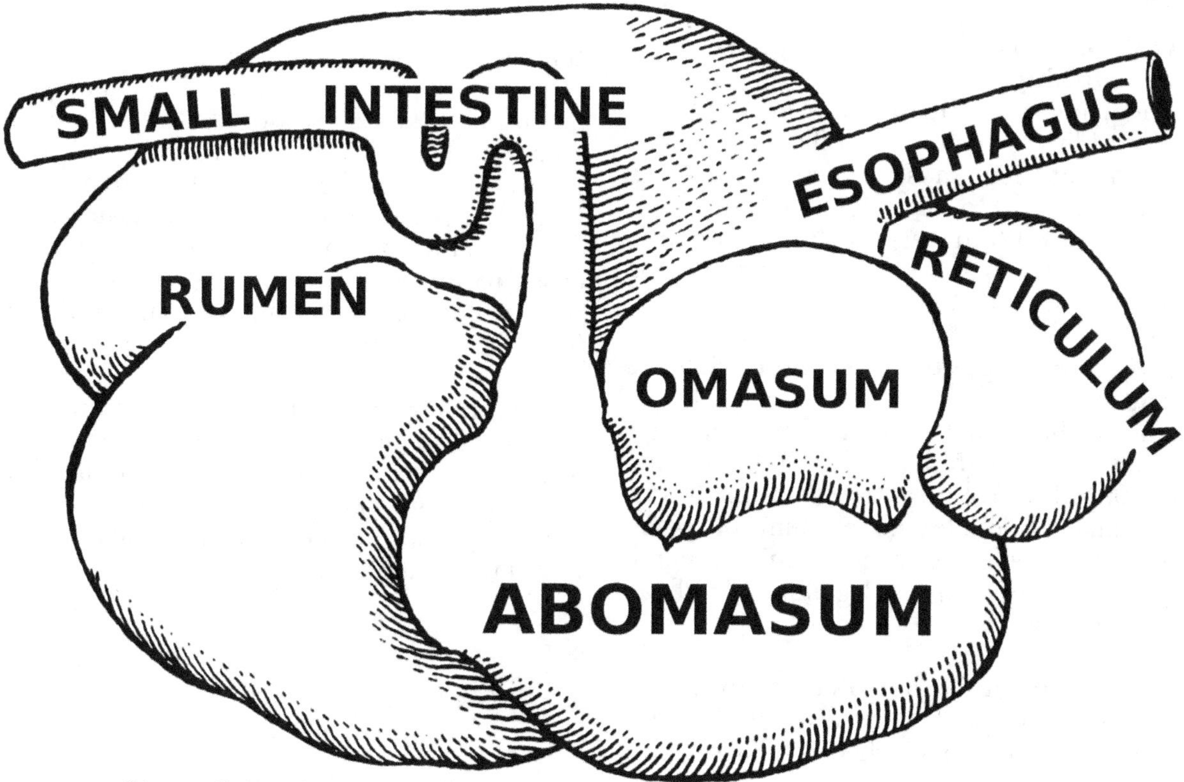

Diagram of baby ruminant stomachs. The abomasum is in between the small intestine and the round omasum.

Rennet paste

How to make rennet paste

To make rennet paste, weigh out some pieces of dried salted abomasum and put them through a food processor or mortar and pestle. Slowly add 8 parts by weight of clean non-chlorinated water and grind it all up into a paste (e.g. for 5 grams of dried abomasum, add 40 grams (1.4oz) water). If your scale won't measure that low, just measure by teaspoons, assuming that 2 teaspoons is 5 grams. Mix through 5% salt by weight (1½ teaspoons for every 100 grams (3.5oz) of finished rennet paste). Keep in the fridge for up to 6 months.

How to use rennet paste in cheesemaking

A standard dose is ½ teaspoon of rennet paste for every 4 litres (1 gallon) of milk, so you'd use this amount for most cheeses, such as mozzarella, feta, Gouda, Cheddar, and more. For chèvre, use 1/8th teaspoon for 4 litres milk. Use up to 1 teaspoon for every 4 litres milk for Alpine cheeses and Parmesan.

To help rennet paste last longer without a fridge

Weigh out the rennet paste, and mix through 50% salt by weight (5 flat tablespoons (50g) for every 100g (3.5oz) of paste). When using this in cheesemaking, double the amount of paste used, so that for most cheeses you're using 1 teaspoon for every 4 litres (1 gallon) of milk as a standard dose.

To make frozen rennet paste tablets

Divide the rennet paste into the amounts you'd normally use for one cheese. Place each amount in an ice cube tray and freeze until solid. Transfer to a jar or a bag and store in the freezer until needed.

How to use dried rennet as-needed for cheesemaking

This is the approach to take if you are not making much cheese, or if you are living without a fridge in warm weather, and want your rennet to last as long as possible. It may take some experimentation to figure out the right amount of natural rennet to use for your cheeses.

Start with a piece roughly a quarter or half a teaspoon in size to set around a gallon (four litres) of milk. Use scissors to cut it into tiny pieces and then put it in a mortar and pestle with a little bit of salt. Smash it many times with the pestle to grind it up. Add water, a tiny amount at a time, using the pestle to mix and crush it further, dilute it in a bit more water, then add it all to your cultured milk and leave for the usual rennetting time.

If it has not set with this amount of rennet, you will need to add more – process the same amount of rennet in the same way as last time, mix it through and see how that works. Once you've figured out the right dose, take note of it and use that amount in future.

Cultures

Raw milk naturally has cultures and helpful bacteria in it that can sometimes create a great cheese all on its own. For the most part, the raw milk cultures are best thought of as aging cultures rather than starter cultures – they add something unique to the aging cheese, but can't always be relied on as a culture to start the culturing process. To make the initial culturing process more predictable, most cheesemakers will use a starter culture of some sort.

Starter cultures are helpful bacteria that convert the lactose in milk into lactic acid. This process can also be called acidification, ripening, or just plain 'culturing'. Starter cultures are usually divided into two categories: mesophilic and thermophilic.

Mesophilic cultures are most active between 21°C to 32°C (70°F-90°F) and are favoured for cheeses that are cultured at lower temperatures.

Thermophilic starter cultures are most active between 40°C and 45°C (104°F-113°F), and are used in cheeses that are heated above 40°C (104°F).

Some natural starter cultures contain both mesophilic and thermophilic cultures, others are more specific.

As well as starter cultures, there are also other helpful bacteria, moulds, and yeasts that contribute to the aging process of a cheese. In natural cheesemaking, these cultures are naturally present where you make and age cheeses, and are encouraged or discouraged depending on the type of cheese made, the aging conditions, and any additional processes taken during aging such as washing rinds, allowing extra humidity to encourage moulds or less humidity to discourage them, a brief stay at a higher temperature to encourage eyes, different salt contents, and more. In low tech cheese aging spaces that are not easily controlled, often some cultures will thrive at certain times of year and not other times.

For making cheese without packaged cultures, the following starter cultures are most commonly used:

Kefir

Kefir is my favourite cheese culture. It contains both mesophilic and thermophilic starter bacteria and can be used in any cheese, it is pretty invincible, and if you forget about it, you can usually bring it back to life again by rinsing well and feeding it (it may need to be rinsed and fed twice or more to be active again).

Real milk kefir comes from milk kefir grains, which look like tiny cauliflowers. Because the culture is in the kefir grains rather than the liquid, it's less likely to get contaminated than liquid cultures, as the kefir grains can be rinsed out every time and fed with fresh milk.

To use kefir for cheesemaking, first rinse your grains really well in cold water, and culture some milk with them - around 1 cup (240ml) of milk to 1 teaspoon of grains. Allow the milk to culture for around 8 to 16 hours, then taste it - it should be pleasantly sour and tasty, but have no unpleasant flavours. If you don't like the taste of it, use the milk in a smoothie, rinse the grains well, and start over again - it may just be that the culture needs to be woken up and won't develop its true flavour until you've made a few batches. Different strains of kefir have different tastes, so if you don't like the first batch of kefir you try, you can experiment with kefir grains from different sources.

You don't have to like the taste of kefir to make cheese from it, but it is best to try and treat it well -

I think of it in some ways as similar to sourdough baking - if I want the best results from my sourdough, I feed it a few hours before using it and feed it often, and if I want the best results from my kefir for cheese culturing, I will rinse and feed the grains, and allow it to culture for several hours before using it.

I find that kefir, like sourdough, really benefits from being brewed often. The best cheeses I've made have been when I've been making fresh kefir every day, so that my kefir grains are very active and will culture the milk quickly. I keep a small jar (around a cup and a half (375ml) in size) with around a teaspoon-sized piece of kefir grains and top it up with fresh raw goats milk every day. This provides enough kefir for a drink every day, while not brewing so much that I can't find a use for it.

Kefir works best with a room temperature of around 74°F (23°C), so if your kitchen is hotter or colder than this, try to find the perfect spot in your house to culture the kefir, which can change throughout the year, for example, in winter I might keep the kefir near my woodstove, and in summer I might keep it further away from the stove. In hot weather, the kefir may separate into curds and whey in 12 hours, and in cold weather, it may take 48 hours to culture the milk sufficiently to make cheese with it. If the weather is consistently hot, it may help to reduce the amount of kefir grains in the milk, to brew larger batches, or to reduce the amount of time it is brewed for. In cold weather it may help to increase the amount of kefir grains in the milk, as well as letting it brew for twice as long as usual.

To get kefir, you can ask around - often there is someone in your circle of friends or community that makes kefir, or you can purchase a dried kefir culture from the internet.

Kefir grains look like tiny cauliflowers

Viili

Viili is a mesophilic room temperature yoghurt culture that is sweet and mild, and when it's working well, makes a good cheese culture (although not as reliable as kefir). Viili also doesn't like to be forgotten about, and prefers to be cultured twice per week (if you have a fridge, you might be able to get away with once a week culturing though). For instructions on how to make viili, see page 121.

Crème fraiche and buttermilk

Like viili, these are mesophilic cultures, thriving at warm room temperature. These make delicious cheeses, but I also find them less reliable than kefir, as they are more easily contaminated by unwanted bacteria. To make your own crème fraiche, see the recipe on page 123.

Yoghurt

A yoghurt with live cultures from the shop will work in recipes that prefer a thermophilic culture, such as alpine cheeses. The fresher the yoghurt is, the better the culture will be. For a yoghurt recipe, see page 122.

Leftover whey

Many traditional cheeses are made with whey leftover from the last batch of cultured cheese. This works really well when cheese is being made every day or two, but the whey becomes less active and more likely to spoil if it is left for longer. To make whey last as long as it possibly can, allow it to sit for a short time, for the milky-looking whey to rise towards the top of the bowl, scoop the milky stuff off and feed it to the chickens, then strain the watery whey through a few layers of cheesecloth. This watery whey will now store for slightly longer, and can also be used as a starter culture for fermented vegetables.

Whey as a starter culture will only work when made with whey from raw cultured cheeses, not from vinegar cheeses such as ricotta, paneer, and fast mozzarella.

Raw milk culture

Raw milk can be soured on its own and then be used to culture a cheese. To achieve this, start with a healthy animal, a very clean udder and a very clean jar. Milk the first three squirts out of the udder onto the ground, to get rid of any unwanted bacteria lurking in the teat, and then milk around a half a cup of milk directly into a 250ml (half pint) jar. Leave the jar with a covering of light cheesecloth, out somewhere where it can be exposed to good bacteria, such as outdoors somewhere pleasant, or on an open airy place within the house. Leave this for 24 to 48 hours at around 18°C (65°F) then taste – is it nicely sour? If there is any kind of off taste, then don't use it, but if it tastes pleasantly sour, this can now be fed in a similar way to a sourdough starter, just remove some of this for your cheese (the same amount as you would use with kefir or whey), and then add in some very clean fresh milk and leave at 18°C (65°F), covered, to culture.

For this culture, as with viili, there is more chance of contamination than there is with kefir, so I prefer to stick with kefir, but if for some reason you were stuck on an island with a herd of goats and no kefir, it's helpful to know that you can harvest a wild culture from the air in this way.

To avoid contaminating your culture, once it's established, you could feed it with pasteurised milk, and the cultures will feed on the milk but the milk won't add anything new of its own. Another option would be just to feed it straight after milking (only if the milk is very clean), as this will give the good cultures in the starter a chance to take over before anything unwanted begins to grow.

For best results, keep your raw milk culture below 20°C (68°F). If you need to store it for longer than two days, store it at fridge temperatures.

How much culture?

All of the above liquid cultures can be added to the milk at roughly 1 tablespoon (15g) for every 1 litre or 1 quart of milk. To simplify the recipes in this book I've only mentioned a couple of options for each cheese, but feel free to change these around to work with whatever natural culture you are using from the above list.

Leftover cheese

If you have a piece of freshly-cut cheese, you can sometimes get cultures from it by slicing it carefully again with a very clean knife, to expose a bit of cheese that no person or wrapper has ever touched, and then breaking this piece of cheese up into a small amount of milk, to culture the milk for a few hours. The cheese bits are then strained out of the milk, and the cultured milk is used to culture the cheese.

There are a lot of 'what ifs' with this method - if you use a cheese that is made from pasteurised milk and cultured with one strain of culture, it might not be the most resilient culture to use and may not work well, but if you use a raw milk cheese, traditionally cultured from leftover whey, then you might be bringing lots of interesting cultures into your cheese. Contamination with unwanted cultures is also an issue, because the cheese has been sitting aging for months, and is not as fresh as whey or freshly-made kefir; anyone that bakes sourdough bread will know that a freshly-fed starter will make better bread - the same is true for cheese cultures, that an active and recently-fed starter will culture your cheese more reliably.

Commercial cultures, and how to perpetuate them at home

Many home cheesemakers begin their journey with packaged cultures. These can be a reliable way to follow a recipe and develop cheesemaking skills, but once the package runs out, more needs to be purchased.

When I used packaged cultures, I never used the single-dose packets that are most commonly found, as they are really expensive. Instead, I bought packet sizes more suited to regular home cheesemaking, kept them in the freezer, and scooped the culture out with a tiny sterilised spoon, and they still worked. It's not something I would go back to now that I've discovered kefir, but is helpful to know about if you have trouble with kefir and other natural cultures.

It is also possible to buy a powdered culture once, and to keep it alive at home. To do this put a litre (1 quart) of pasteurised milk in a sterilised jar, warm it to cheesemaking temperature, mix through ¼ teaspoon of powdered culture, and leave it to culture, with a lid on, for 24 hours at cheesemaking temperature (around 32°C (90°F) for mesophilic culture, a bit warmer for thermophilic.

At the end of the culturing time, the milk should be thickened considerably, and should smell like cultured milk. This cultured milk is added to the cheese at the same rate as kefir and viili, one tablespoon to 1 litre (1 quart) of milk.

Once cultured, divide it up into smaller amounts, using a sterilised ice cube tray or similar, freeze it, and keep it in a freezer for later use. When you need a new batch, you can use this frozen culture to re-culture a new batch of pasteurised milk.

Powdered cultures are not very resilient - they are a

single strain of finicky bacteria, and they can get upset if they are fed with raw milk and its natural cultures. You can still use these cultures in raw milk cheeses, but pasteurised milk is used for keeping the culture alive.

Salt

My recipes are developed to be made with unrefined salts without additives. You can make this at home by boiling seawater in a pan until it evaporates, and many unrefined salts can be purchased in shops or online, such as Himalayan salt or Celtic sea salt. I use finely ground unrefined salts for my recipes.

If you can't find unrefined salts, you can use plain sea salt or rock salt without additives, dairy salt, pickling salt, or flossy salt. These salts are higher in sodium and taste saltier than mineral-rich unrefined salts, so less is needed - reducing the amount of salt in a recipe to ¾ teaspoon for every teaspoon called for is recommended if you want to use these refined salts.

Iodised salt, or salt with anti-caking agents and other additives will negatively impact your cheeses, so always check the ingredients list to make sure there isn't anything strange added.

Some cheesemakers soak their hard cheeses in a saturated brine to salt them, but I find on a home scale it is much easier to just rub salt all over the cheese instead. The rate of salt to rub on is usually around 1 standard US/UK tablespoon (10g) of unrefined salt for every 1 gallon (4 litres) of milk used in the recipe.

The ideal amount of salt for each cheese varies slightly, see the section on salting on page 56 for more information.

Cheesemaking Equipment

There is a lot of fuss over what equipment you *need* to begin cheesemaking. In reality, what you actually need will depend on what kind of cheeses you want to make and have time to make. It's easy to get overambitious at first and to get everything that a list tells you that you need to get, but often it makes sense to just start with the basics, use what you already have as much as possible, and grow your cheesemaking collection as your cheese skills grow.

Basic cheesemaking equipment

Something to culture your milk in
This needs to be something non-reactive. Avoid aluminium. For chèvre and small batch Camembert I just use mason jars. For larger cheeses I use stainless steel pots.

My favourite cheesemaking pot has a heavy base, and a lid without any air vents. Pots with vent holes in the lid can allow unwanted stuff to get into the cheese while it's culturing. If all your pots have vents in the lids, covering it with a tea towel when it's not on the stove will help.

I avoid using enamelled pots for cheesemaking because they can get scratched while cutting into the curds or stirring with a metal spoon.

For the best results with curd cutting, it helps to choose a pot that will only just hold your milk, as this makes it easier to get the curd knife as horizontal as possible. I use either a five litre or a ten litre pot, depending on how much milk I'm working with.

A long-handled spoon
A slotted spoon is handy to have for diluting rennet and draining the curds, and I use mine for stirring the curds as well, but you can also just use any non-plastic spoon. You probably don't want to use a wooden spoon that has the scent of curries or onion soup on it, but a wooden spoon that you keep just for cheesemaking, porridge, and other non-smelly stuff will be fine.

A long-handled wooden spoon or spatula is handy to have for hanging up chèvre and other cheeses that are hung up to drain.

A ramekin or small jar for diluting rennet, a teaspoon or syringe, and a fork
You probably already have these things.

A knife for cutting curds
I once owned a specialist curd-cutting knife, but it got packed in the bottom of a box when I moved to a kitchen with no storage space and since then I've been getting along fine with my usual kitchen chef knife for curd cutting, even though it is not ideal. Any long knife that can easily be sterilised with boiling water will work for this. For Alpine cheeses I use a large balloon whisk to cut the curds.

A cloth to strain curds in
I use an unbleached organic cotton cheesecloth from a place called 'Country Trading' that is fairly easy to find online at the time I write this, but non-fluffy tea towels can be used instead, or just any bit of non-toxic fabric such as cotton or linen (do not use hessian - it is not safe for food). The type of cloth you use will impact how readily the curds drain - some are so tightly woven that it will take a long time to drain, or won't drain all the whey,

some are so loose that you'll lose some of your curds, so it can be worth putting in some effort to find the right one. Cheesecloths labelled as "butter muslin" tend to be the right weave for cheesemaking. Cheesecloth, if well cared for, can last a long time. I usually just pick any bits of cheese off the cloth straight after using, rinse it in cool water, and then hang outside on the washing line to dry and bleach in the sun.

Cheesecloth usually comes in one big piece. When I need a new piece, I just cut off a square the right size and use that, not worrying about any fraying at the ends. Cheesecloth tends to shrink while being washed, so it's best to cut a slightly larger square than needed to make up for this. To find the right size for cheeses, I line the cheese mould with it, allowing a little extra to overhang on the edges, and then cut out just enough to completely fill the cheese mould with a little extra to fold on top.

Whatever the type of cloth you choose to use, it is a good idea to soak it in warm whey before straining your cheese through it - adjusting the pH of the cloth in this way makes the cheese drain more readily, and helps to avoid the curds sticking to the cloth.

To clean cheesecloth, just rinse it well in cold or lukewarm water shortly after cheesemaking to remove all traces of curds and whey, and then hang out to dry. Do not wash cheesecloth with your regular laundry washing or use soaps or detergents of any kind, as the cheesecloth can pick up smells and tastes from anything it is washed with, and give unwanted flavours to the cheese.

A colander (or bowl)
A colander is lined with cheesecloth and used to place curds in while you tie the corners of the cheesecloth up to drain a soft cheese, and sometimes it is used in hard cheese recipes to pre-drain the curds.

It's best if any colanders and bowls used are easy to sterilise, and non-reactive. Stainless steel is usually a good choice. Avoid aluminium.

With the above equipment, you can make chèvre, ricotta, paneer, yoghurt cheese, feta, mozzarella and aged chèvre such as crottin.

Advanced cheesemaking equipment

Maybe a dairy thermometer, or learn to read temperature with your wrist
If you don't mind a bit of "it depends" working its way into your cheesemaking times, you can live without a thermometer. It's also possible to guess the temperature with the inside of your wrist. A long thermometer with a clip, such as the one pictured on page 37 is good to have if you want to have accurate cheesemaking times. For all types of cheesemaking, a simple dairy or coffee thermometer that goes from 0°C to 100°C (32°F to 212°F) is the best choice, as you'll want to see readings close to 32°C (90°F) for culturing, up to 50°C (122°F) for heating the curds, and up to around 90°C (194°F) for ricotta and paneer.

I used my thermometer for every cheese when I was learning, I later went for a time of not bothering at all. These days I use it for many hard cheeses, but not for chèvre.

Thermometers are not always accurate. You can test the accuracy by immersing it it in icy water and checking the reading, which will read very close to 0°C or 32°F if it's accurate. If you're close to sea level, you can also test it in rolling boiling water, which should read 100°C or 212°F, but this test will not work at high altitudes.

You can also follow the instructions below for reading temperature with your wrist, checking the thermometer readings against these.

To learn how to read the temperature of cheese with your wrist, it's useful to have a thermometer, and to see what the milk feels like when it's at various temperatures. Without a thermometer it's useful to get to know what 'lukewarm', or around 32°C (90°F) feels like - to me, this feels like it can only just be called 'warm' - if you imagine there is a scale from cold, to cool, to lukewarm, to bath-temperature warm, to washing dishes warm, and then hot, and to be observant, you'll be able to notice when the milk changes from cool into a temperature that could only just slightly be called warm - this is the ideal temperature for culturing and rennetting most cheeses.

Hard cheeses usually get heated up after the curd has been cut, if you don't have a thermometer you can guess the temperatures and allow a bit of extra time if you'd prefer to keep it too cool rather than too hot. Testing the temperature during heating with the inside of your wrist, you can judge when it feels too hot - if you can't hold your wrist in there comfortably for longer than a few seconds, it's heated enough. With a cooked curd cheese, you can make the same observation with a finger, which has a lower sensitivity than the wrist – if it feels too hot to hold your finger in there for longer than a few seconds, then it's hot enough. In general it's better to err on the side of too cool, rather than risk cooking all the cultured goodness out of your cheese, but the wrist and finger temperatures can be fairly reliable indicators if you're observing the temperature often.

Cheese mould (aka cheese basket)

Cheese moulds can be made out of food-safe containers such as yoghurt buckets, if you can find one the right size. For small batch cheesemaking I like to use a specialty cheese mould designed to hold up to 800g (28oz) of curds. This size mould measures 12cm (4 and 3/4 inches) in diameter, 13.5cm (5 and 1/4 inches) high, and works well for me for making cheese from 1 to 2 gallons (4 to 8 litres) of milk, as well as making one Camembert from 2 litres (half a gallon) of milk.

If you want to avoid specialty cheese moulds, keep an eye out for a straight-sided food-grade bucket less than 1 litre (1 quart) in size. You may be able to find one used to package yoghurt, feta cheese, or dips, just make sure it is taller than it is wide, and that the sides are very straight. To turn it into a cheese mould, drill or punch small holes all around the sides and base, making sure the inside surface is smooth.

For hard cheeses you need to have a follower for your cheese mould - this is a disc that fits neatly inside the cheese mould, which the weight or cheese press will sit on. Most hard cheese moulds come with a follower, but if they don't, you can fashion one from a few yoghurt bucket lids with the edges trimmed down to make a completely flat surface, or with a thicker piece of wood or plastic.

For Camembert and blue cheese it is handy to have open bottomed cylinder-type moulds, but this is not essential if you can be careful when flipping. If you want to make something yourself, keep an eye out for plastic jars used to package foods, removing the base and trimming it down as needed to form a straight cylinder. Punch or drill holes all around the sides, making sure to keep the inside surface of the cylinder smooth.

Ways to press cheeses

The purpose of pressing a cheese is to get the curds to knit together, to expel more whey, and to allow the cheese to continue culturing and acidifying. Most cheeses can do this without a cheese press.

Observation is key to understanding how much weight is actually needed. The first press is usually done for 15 to 30 minutes, and due to the shrinkage of the curds in the cheesecloth, the outside of the cheese can appear to be quite bumpy and wrinkled after this. A second pressing can also be made quite short – after half an hour you can check on the cheese again and observe whether the outside is starting to look smooth. If there is still a lot of bumpiness to the sides and it still looks like a bunch of curds ready to fall to bits, feel free to add more weight now.

Adding the right amount of weight early on, while the cheese is still quite warm will help it to expel whey more efficiently without a cheese press.

Some cheeses, such as Cheddar, are put under a lot of pressure, others are happy with just a quart jar filled with water. With smaller batches of cheese the challenge is to find a way to press the cheeses that will fit inside your small cheese mould.

One way of pressing cheeses in a small mould is to find a block of wood that will fit inside the cheese mould and stick out a decent amount above it, and then to find something to weigh this down - either using pressure from those tie-down straps that are used to keep things secured on trucks, or with dumbbell weights plates.

My Fowlers canning jars, and 1 quart mason jars, will fit inside my small cheese mould – I will sometimes do the first pressing with a full #27 jar, and then the second pressing with a full #36 jar. When using jars, it's helpful to be draining your cheese in a sink, so that if the jars end up toppling, they don't have far to fall.

Speciality cheese presses are available from cheesemaking supply shops. I use one sometimes and like it. I have little people running about in my kitchen that will easily send a pile of weights plates and other inventive solutions tumbling down and hurting someone, so I like that my cheese press is pretty simple and un-wreckable. If I were starting over now, I wouldn't buy one, and would be content just making the types of hard cheeses that don't need much weight, such as tomme, Alpine, and Havarti. The only times I use my cheese press these days are if I am making Cheddar, or if the curds of my jar-pressed cheeses have become too hard and dry and are not knitting together under the usual amount of weight, which only really happens if I've let the stirring process go on for too long.

How to use gentle heat during the cheesemaking process

Some cheesemakers make their cheese by creating a double boiler with two large pots, or by using a pot in a water-filled sink, so that the outside pot or sink can contain hot water, and the inside pot of milk can heat very slowly without being scorched on the bottom.

The Gouda style of cheese was developed by people who used wooden cheese vats - the only way to heat the curd was to replace the whey with hot water, so the vat was never heated directly.

Many home cheesemakers use a stainless steel pot for heating their cheeses. Pots with heavy bases will help to avoid hot spots and scorched curds, but more care is still needed than with the double boiler method, as the direct heat from the stove is harsher than a double boiler.

For most cheeses, I use the coolest edge of my wood stove, moving the pot between there and the kitchen bench to heat it up slowly. Whenever it is on the stove, I make sure I am around to watch and stir it.

When I used an electric stove, I would have the hotplate or burner on the very lowest setting, switching it off and on every so often, to get the temperature to rise slowly. When making a cooked curd cheese such as Emmental or Gruyère, it's very important to stir often if you are using bottom heat from a hotplate, burner, or woodstove, to make sure that the curds are heating up and losing whey evenly.

If you're using the double boiler method, considerations for this are to create it in such a way that you don't risk splashing your cheese with water, and to also be conscious of the times stated in the cheese recipe, checking your water temperature and refilling it with warmer water (or putting it on the stovetop) when needed. If the outer pot gets too hot, you can always remove your cheese pot from it once you've reached a stage where you just need to maintain temperature. When the cheese recipe says to hold your cheese pot at a certain temperature for a while, for example when culturing, or during a recipe that is stirred but not heated, having water the same temperature (or slightly higher) than your cheese pot temperature will help buffer it from the impact of the cool air.

When a cheese is heated over a period of time, it's important to keep to that time, and not to rush it, especially early on in the process, as this can cause the curds to lose whey unevenly and to trap whey inside. If you're not sure, just heat as slow as possible for the first half of the heating, and then once the curds have begun to shrink, you can get away with heating more quickly for the second half of the heating time, just make sure you are around to stir frequently during this time.

Cheese press, 800g cheese mould with follower, dairy thermometer, slotted spoon, and cheesecloth. With these tools you can make any cheese, but all you need to get started with soft cheese is the cheesecloth.

Learning to Make Cheese, Step by Step

1. Make ricotta and paneer
The best way to demonstrate the wonder of cheese is to make a simple ricotta or paneer. I like to use this as a first lesson when I'm teaching cheesemaking, just to show how easy it can be.

This may not be the first cheese we think of when we think about cheese, but learning to make ricotta at home means we can make cheesecake, and all kinds of sweet and savoury tarts and pies. Ricotta can also be mashed up with some eggs and vegetables and made into patties and fritters.

Paneer can be used in curries, stir fries, and sandwiches. Often rather than bothering to make halloumi, I will just make paneer and fry that up instead. A sandwich of homemade pickles with fried paneer is a quick meal that makes the most of milk as a staple food.

2. Make a simple soft cheese
There is a saying that the harder a cheese is in texture, the harder it is to make. Soft cheeses can be made with pretty much no hands-on time - just shake the milk with the culture and rennet in a jar, leave it until set, and drain. Soft cheeses are at their best when very fresh, so are excellent ones to make as home, as your homemade ones will always be better than ones from the shop.

3. Try out feta and fast mozzarella
Feta and fast mozzarella are easy and rewarding to make, and they also help develop the cheesemaking skills of gently stirring and heating curds, and feeling the texture of the curds to see when they're ready - both of these skills are essential for making harder cheeses, but these two cheeses are ready very soon, so you can soon taste whether they have worked out or not.

4. Make one of the easier hard cheeses.
Tomme, Havarti and Gouda are all fast-aging cheeses where you can learn about what is growing on the natural rinds, and whether your aging conditions will be suitable for bloomy white and blue cheeses. Being able to age a cheese for just one or two months means that you can quickly learn whether you'd like to make a particular cheese again or not.

5. Make any other cheese you'd like
By now, if you've been observant, you will have a better feel for making cheese, and the way that surface ripening and aging works. Sometimes it can take a while before you become confident with it, but at some point you will be able to make cheese without a recipe, and might come up with some unique cheeses of your own.

Finding cheeses that work for you

Busy schedule, not in the kitchen much.
Try chèvre and aged chèvres. These cheeses have simple steps that are spaced many hours apart, so it's possible to start it culturing at breakfast, drain it before bed, and salt it at breakfast the next day, and then shape it or put it in jars later that day. Have a look at the time section of the other cheese recipes to find other cheeses that can fit into your schedule. Camembert and Brie don't need stirring and have some flexibility.

Havarti and Gouda are somewhat tolerant of neglect, as it's easy with the washed curd process to control the buildup of acid. Cheeses that aren't heated during stirring, such as feta and blue cheese are more tolerant of being left alone than heated cheeses.

Fast cheeses, such as ricotta, paneer, and fast mozzarella are all easily made on the stovetop in minimal time.

Want to preserve milk for the winter without much trouble
Try tomme, Havarti, Gouda, and feta for storage in cheese cave conditions (feta can also be stored in a fridge). Ricotta, paneer, mozzarella and chèvre can be frozen. Alpine cheeses can be quite simple to make and store well in a cheese cave.

Nowhere suitable to age cheeses
Try aging feta in an unheated room (or in the fridge). Feta is aged in a jar so there's no need to worry about humidity or rodents. Focus on freshly-made cheeses such as mozzarella, ricotta, paneer, and chèvre, all of which can be frozen for later if needed.

If you have a rodent-free place to age cheeses but it is a bit too warm (at around 18°C (64°F) instead of 15°C (59°F) or less), you can age Parmesan-style grating cheeses.

Want to make basic cheeses to feed the family
Try fast mozzarella. Ricotta for cheesecakes, tarts, and veggie burgers. Chèvre because it's so simple and tasty. Try simple hard cheeses such as Havarti or tomme to use as everyday slicing or grating cheeses.

Cheesemaking schedules, and how to fit cheesemaking into life

The information below is based on a typical hard cheese. Some cheeses are much more flexible.

Feeding the culture
In warm weather, I feed my kefir culture the night before I make cheese. If my kitchen is cold, I will feed the kefir 24 to 48 hours before I begin the cheese.

Culturing
The culturing time of the cheese is hands-off – you an even lengthen it if you use strategies later on to reduce the buildup of acid, such as washed curd and cooked curd techniques. Cheeses are usually cultured for between 30 minutes and 3 hours, depending on the recipe. If you need to lengthen the culturing time, try to reduce the temperature.

Rennetting
If you have left your milk culturing for longer than stated in the recipe, be near the cheese for this stage and cut as soon as clean break is achieved, which may be as low as 10 minutes for very fresh milk. If

you've left your cheese culturing for the normal culturing time, rennet can be left for longer if needed. Larger curds don't mind being cut after a longer wait, small curds prefer to be cut closer to the time of clean break. As with culturing, if you leave your cheese in this stage for longer-than-ideal, you can take steps later on to reduce the buildup of acidity.

Cutting and stirring
This is the time to be in the kitchen, especially if you are making a cooked curd cheese. The curd is cut, and usually left alone for five to ten minutes, and then afterwards it should be stirred roughly every five minutes.

First press
For best results, make sure you will be there 20 to 30 minutes after the first press starts, so that you can begin the second press.

Second and further pressings
This is quite flexible. The ideal cheese pressing temperature is around 21°C (70°F), so if you need to lengthen this pressing, you can press at a cooler temperature, which will reduce the buildup of acidity in the cheese. I would always prefer to have a longer pressing rather than trying to hurry this up, but if for some reason you need to hurry it up slightly, try to keep the temperature at around 24°C (75°F).

Salting
Unless salt has been added directly to to the curds, such as for Cheddar, once all the pressings are done, salting is done to halt the development of acidity and to help avoid unwanted moulds growing on the surface. If you delay this stage by an hour or two, it's not going to make a huge difference, just don't delay it for days on end.

In a homesteader's schedule, based on needing to be in the kitchen to do meal cooking and kitchen chores at a certain time of day, what this might look like would be:

The day before: feed kefir grains with fresh milk
1 ½ hours before cooking: culture the cheese
½ hour before cooking: add rennet
While cooking the meal: cut and stir curds, start first pressing
½ hour after leaving the kitchen: second pressing

From all this, we can gather that hard cheesemaking is best done when the cheesemaker is at home. On busy days away from the house, it makes more sense to make chèvre, or to make a quick vinegar cheese such as ricotta, paneer, or mozzarella, or to store the milk for the next day.

Being aware of how my schedule impacts my cheesemaking has helped me to make more cheese. When I see it as a serious part of our self sufficiency, I can fit it into my kitchen chores while I am cooking meals and preserving food. I plan to make chèvre when we are going out for the day, hard cheeses when I will be in the kitchen, and vinegar cheeses when I have a smaller amount of milk or when I've been too busy earlier in the day to make hard cheese.

Observing your cheese needs helps. If you like to make pizza once a week, making a batch of mozzarella once a week will make sense. If you like lots of hard cheeses, make sure to find time to regularly make that. If you find that you're making too much of one type of cheese, either find more ways to eat that, or prioritise other cheesemaking instead.

For an example, this might be what I might do with the milk in one week, if we are getting 5 litres a day (5 quarts):
Monday: Make yoghurt, store some milk for tomorrow drinking, feed kefir.
Tuesday: Make hard cheese (Havarti), start tiny batch gjetost, feed kefir.
Wednesday: Going out. Make chèvre, store some milk for tomorrow's drinking, feed kefir.
Thursday: Make hard cheese (Alpine), make gjetost, maybe feed kefir.
Friday: Make yoghurt, store some milk for tomorrow's drinking, maybe feed kefir.
Saturday: Make mozzarella, maybe feed kefir.
Sunday: Make paneer, feed kefir.

I am not usually so organised as to have it all mapped out like it is above, but to plan things one day in advance, I know to store the drinking milk away so that I can use all the next day's milk fresh for cheese. I know that if I want to make yoghurt, It's best to plan that for a non-cheesemaking day. When we are going out, I know that's the day to make chèvre. We are not bringing huge amounts of milk in, but I am providing cheese in many forms as a staple part of our homegrown diet.

Understanding the cheesemaking process

What we are doing when making any kind of cheese is acidifying the milk (usually by cultures that feed on lactose and convert it into lactic acid), separating it into curds and whey (usually with the help of rennet), and removing varying amounts of whey, to turn highly perishable milk into a solid food that stores for longer.

Making any kind of cultured and rennetted cheese involves roughly the same ingredients and steps, with the addition of aging for some cheeses. The first step is the culturing of the milk.

If you just want to quickly go on to making your first simple soft cheese, feel free to skip this section where I explain the entire process. If you want to understand how and why it all works please read on!

Cleaning and preparing

Before making a cheese I think it's a good idea to get all sourdough and kombucha (and anything else with yeast in it) away from where the cheese will be made, to stop the yeasts getting into the cheese. I keep these on the other side of the kitchen, and will either begin the cheese before I begin the bread (while keeping the lid on the cheese), or I will make sure the bread has been mixed a while before I start the cheesemaking, so that there aren't any stray bits of yeast or flour floating around after kneading. I make sourdough bread, so there is probably less risk of yeasts floating around with this than there is with yeast bread.

With all the above said, milk kefir actually does contain some yeasts. Yeasts generally prefer to feast on flour and don't aggressively take over milk, but it can't hurt to be careful.

It's important to have clean hands. Soap and water will do a good job.

Most cheesemakers like to sterilise anything that will touch the cheese. I do this by bringing my cheesemaking pot with some water in it to the boil with my slotted spoon inside it and my thermometer attached. I rotate the pot around to coat all the surfaces in boiling water, then pour the water into my heatproof measuring jug that I use for diluting rennet, along with any spoons I will be using. Later on I will usually bring another small pot of water to the boil for sterilising the cheesecloth, colander, whey catching bowl, cheese mould and follower. Sterilising anything oven-proof in an oven heated to around 110°C (230°F) is also an option. There have been times when I haven't bothered to do all of this and it's worked out fine, so it's not essential, but I'd recommend it if you don't want any nasty surprises with unwanted things getting into your cheese.

Water for diluting the rennet with, or washing the curds in the case of Gouda and Havarti needs to also be prepared. If your water is chlorinated, standing it out overnight uncovered should get rid of the chlorine. If your water might have bad bacteria in it, boiling it and then allowing it to cool to room temperature is a good idea.

In general, earlier in the cheesemaking process it is more important to have things clean and/or sterile. Milk is an excellent medium for all kinds of wanted and unwanted bacteria to grow, and as the milk transforms into something more acidic and more solid, the conditions become less and less favourable for competing bacteria.

Culturing

Raw milk contains many beneficial cultures already, but to speed the process of cheesemaking up, and make the fermentation more reliable and less likely to be contaminated by unwanted bacteria, a starter is added. A starter can be fresh whey from a previously successful batch of cheese, room temperature yoghurt such as viili, milk kefir, or dehydrated starter cultures. You can also get away with using yoghurt from the shop if it has live cultures, usually this kind of yoghurt will work best in cooked curd cheese recipes and other recipes that are fermented at higher temperatures, as these cultures aren't very active at the lower temperatures used for most cheeses.

For the home cheese maker aiming towards sustainable cheesemaking, milk kefir made from milk kefir grains is ideal, as it can be fed in small amounts in a similar way to a sourdough starter, and you're not obliged to use it right away for cheese, as is the case with whey. Kefir makes tasty and healthy smoothies, can be used in place in buttermilk in recipes, and it's a nice drink on its own, so it's often worth keeping this culture on hand even if you don't want to make cheese. Follow my recipe for milk kefir on page 120 to make your own.

Cultures are at their best when freshly fed, so if you haven't fed your kefir for a while, make sure to make a fresh batch around 12 to 24 hours before making cheese, and to taste it to make sure it has cultured correctly. Sometimes it can be much slower in cold weather and is best used after 48 hours, and in hot weather it can be ready in 8 hours, so taste it first to make sure. Milk kefir is generally more resilient to being forgotten about than viili and other yoghurts.

Many home cheese makers begin their journey by using dehydrated starter cultures. The benefit of these cultures is that they can just stay in the freezer and come out when you're ready to make cheese, so they need no feeding or extra care, but the downsides are that their packaging is wasteful, they are made in labs far away from where we live, using questionable methods, and their use cannot be sustained over the long term. It's not something like a sourdough starter, yoghurt, or milk kefir that can just be fed again and again from kitchen ingredients. When the packet runs out, more culture needs to be purchased.

Whatever your choice of culture, it is added to milk at the right temperature for the cheese recipe, usually a warm room temperature (I often use milk still slightly warm from the udder as soon as I finish the morning homestead chores). It should not be cold to the touch, but too much heat will kill the cultures. Cheese is traditionally made in some areas by mixing the warm milk fresh from the udder with roughly the same amount of cold milk from the night before to create the ideal temperature for many cheeses. The temperature doesn't need to be exact, but a temperature that is a little colder than in the recipe will mean the culturing stage will take longer; a little warmer (as long as it's not so warm that it kills the culture) will result in faster culturing, and sometimes growing different cultures to the ones that grow at lower temperatures – if you are using kefir or raw cheese whey this is not an issue (these contain thermophilic cultures as well as the lower temperature mesophilic cultures) but if you're using freeze dried mesophilic culture, too much heat will result in unreliable culturing. Too cold a temperature and the cheese will be very slow to culture, and the rennet won't be very active. You can make a cheese without a thermometer if you allow plenty of time and observation for the cheese to get to the right stages. "Baby bath temperature" can be found by touching the milk with the inside of your wrist: If it seems hot, then it's too hot, if it's pleasantly warm, or just slightly lukewarm, then it's fine to begin the cheese recipe.

When the milk is culturing, it is being populated with the helpful bacteria that give cheese flavour while developing the right amount of acidity to work with the rennet to form curds.

The time the milk is cultured for will depend on the cheese you're making, and your schedule. For hard cheeses this is usually somewhere between 30 and 60 minutes, but this can be extended for two hours (and sometimes longer) if needed, so long as you either reduce the culturing temperature, speed the rest of the cheesemaking process up, or use the washed curd method to reduce acidity.

Rennetting

To add rennet to the cheese, it is first diluted in cool water, and then gently sprinkled over the cultured milk before being thoroughly mixed through for one to four minutes in an up and down motion, to ensure that the rennet is evenly distributed throughout the cultured milk and not just stirred into the top.

The length of time you stir for will depend on the milk: If you are using goats milk, stirring for just long enough to confidently mix the rennet through all the milk is fine. For cows milk, the cream can begin to rise to the top while the rennet is settling, so it's a good idea to stir for longer – three minutes is fine.

The cheese mixture is then left alone at the right temperature until the milk separates into curds and whey. The time this will take depends on the recipe, the temperature, and also the amount of rennet and culture added, along with how potent the rennet and culture being used are. Lightly cultured chèvres and other soft cheeses are often left for twelve hours or longer to form a soft curd, the rennet is often added at the same time as the culture in these recipes. Most cheese recipes use a higher dose of rennet and will have this stage lasting less than an hour.

For cheese that is cut into smaller pieces, especially cheeses cut with a whisk such as Alpine cheeses, it's best to observe the rennetting process closely and cut the curds as soon as clean break is achieved, which can be as low as 10 minutes when working with very fresh milk.

For curds that are cut into larger pieces, the rennetting time is more flexible, with an hour or more being good for very large pieces, or 30 to 45 minutes for medium-sized pieces.

It's important that once you have diluted your rennet in water it is added to the milk within half an hour, or the rennet will start to lose its effectiveness. For best results, dilute it right before adding it.

The cheese is not ready for the next stage until a 'clean break' is achieved. To test for this, put a very clean finger or knife diagonally into the curd for around an inch, then gently rip it up through the curd. The curd will still be fairly soft at this stage, but should be strong enough to hold an edge when tested in this way, rather than disintegrating into tiny pieces, and the whey should be separate from the curd. It should be clear, not milky. Leave it for a longer time if it doesn't break cleanly, and check that the temperature is still warm enough (rennet is most active at around 90°F/32°C). If it is taking a very long time, you may want to try gently stirring through some more diluted rennet, and allowing it more time to set.

The amount of rennet to use can vary depending on which type you have, so it's best to check your source of rennet first to find out how much is normally used. For dry rennet in tablet or powder form, cheeses will normally use 1/4 tablet or $1/32^{nd}$ of a teaspoon for every gallon (4 litres) of milk. For strong liquid rennet, 1/4 teaspoon is the usual dose to add for every gallon (4 litres) of milk. Very hard cheeses will use a bit more than this standard amount, and chèvre will use a lot less.

Experience is always the best guide to help decide how much rennet to add. Certain times of the year you may need to use more rennet or less rennet, the information on the packet is not always correct, or your rennet may be getting older and less active.

If you are having trouble with getting your curds to set, consider your water source: Water for diluting rennet should not be alkaline, chlorinated, or chloraminated. For alkaline water, add a drop of non-raw vinegar to the water to increase the acidity, for chlorinated, either a choose a different water source, leave your rennetting water sitting out uncovered overnight to help the chlorine to evaporate, or mix a drop of milk into the water and allow it to sit for a couple of minutes before adding rennet. If your water is chloraminanted, you may have to use a different water source for rennet, or add a drop of milk to your water and allow it to sit, as you might for chlorinated water.

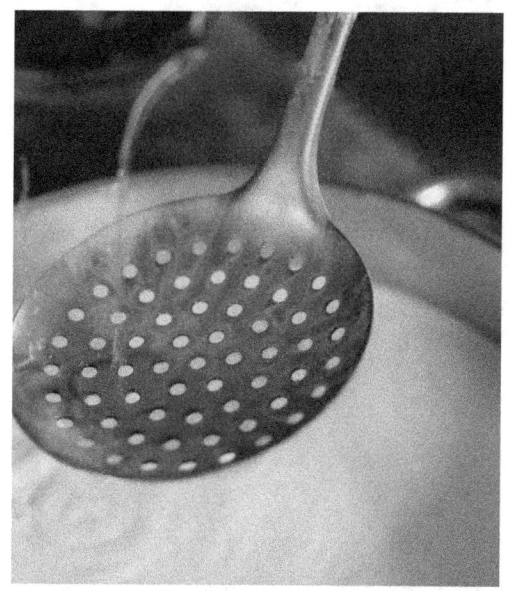

Pouring diluted rennet through the slotted spoon into the cheese pot to evenly distribute it.

Above, 1. Stirring rennet with an up and down motion.

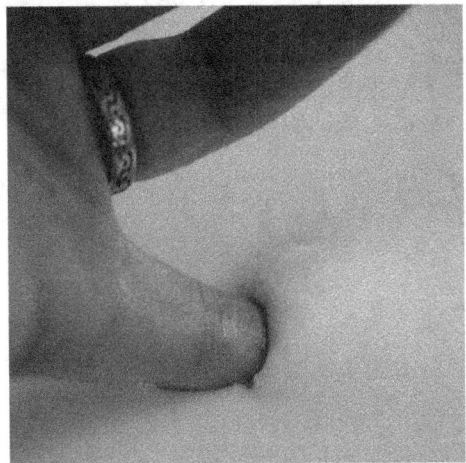

Above, 2. putting my finger diagonally into the curd, to test for clean break

Below, 3. Just ready for an alpine cheese. For most cheeses I'd want it to look cleaner, but for cutting tiny Alpine curds this is fine.

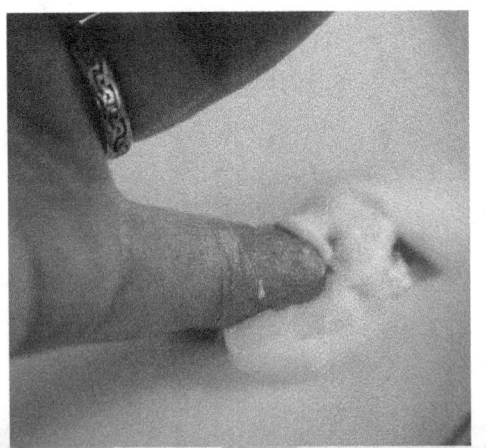

4. The aftermath of the clean break test: The curds are distinct from the whey, with no tiny pieces floating around. Ready for cutting Alpine cheese curds with a whisk.

Above and below, clean break test done with a knife on a cheese with a longer rennetting time.

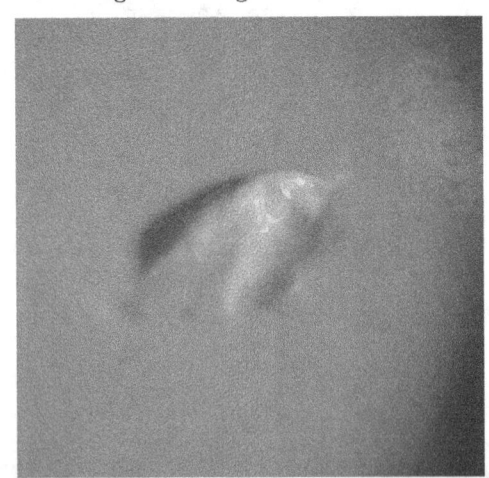

Additional steps, and what they mean

After the rennet has caused the curds to set, soft cheeses are often just placed in cheesecloth to drain, with salt added later. Most cheeses have additional steps, usually involving cutting and stirring the curds, to release whey, increase the acidity, and change the texture of the curds. These steps are usually what makes each cheese so unique.

Cutting the curds

Most cheeses, except the very soft lactic curd cheeses such as chèvre, go through this stage. When the rennet has set the cheese, a long knife is often used to cut the curd roughly into cubes. The knife is first used vertically, to cut through the curds so that the surface is covered in squares, then the knife is used diagonally, to try and cut these square strips into cubes. It's best to let the curds rest for around a minute before beginning the diagonal cut, the curds are very fragile at this stage, and it helps them to not break into tiny pieces. The size of the curds will depend on the recipe; very hard cheeses will cut the curd into tiny pieces, sometimes using a whisk, while softer cheeses such as Brie and Camembert will use much larger curds.

For success with cutting small curds, observe and wait for the clean break, and cut as soon as possible after that. For larger curds, waiting a bit longer is fine.

On a home scale, it is hard to get the curds to be exact squares. The important thing about the curd cutting process is to try and make sure that the curds are all an even size, so that they will lose whey at roughly the same amount.

Some ways to improve the diagonal-cut process can be to use a pot that only just holds your milk, so that you can fit more of the knife in the pot at an angle. You could also look into fashioning a curd cutting knife that does not have a handle – just a thin strip of stainless steel.

If your cheese batch is quite small compared to the wide pot that you're using, you may even be able to get away with making vertical cuts at a right angle to the first set of vertical cuts, the curds formed may be slightly more rectangular than square, but they will all be roughly the same size, and that is what matters.

Any extra-large curds that escaped the knife can be broken in half with a clean hand during the stirring phase.

Once the curds are cut, it's best to allow them to rest for at least five minutes before stirring or any other step, as they are still quite fragile at this stage.

Above and below, cutting Alpine curds with a large balloon whisk.

Above, Curds cut with whisk and ready for stirring. Below, Cutting curds with a knife at an angle.

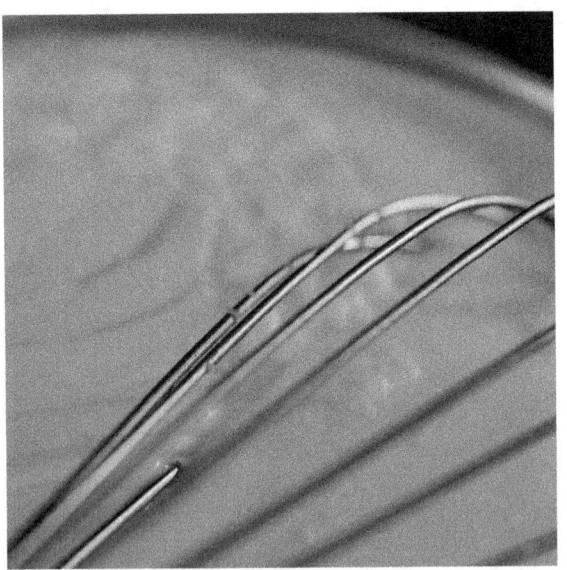

Stirring the curds

Most cheeses that have had their curds cut will then be stirred to release more whey. The time this will take, the temperature, and how it will be handled will depend on the cheese being made.

Most of the time, the curds are heated slowly as they are stirred, to encourage the curds to shrink and expel whey, usually to somewhere between 37°C (99°F) and 43°C (110°F).

Some cheeses are "cooked curd" cheeses and are slowly heated up while being stirred. The "cooking" process involves heating the curds up to 46°C (115°F) or higher. The "cooking" cooks the lactose, sometimes creating delicious caramelised nutty flavours in the cheese (especially with cows milk), this also slows the development of acid by the starter culture, giving a more pliable texture to the cheese. The cooking is not done at such a high temperature as to pasteurise the cheese, so all the raw milk cultures remain intact and ready for more flavour development during draining and aging.

During heating, it's important to heat slowly and gently, especially during the first half of the heating time. Heating too rapidly can result in the outsides of the curds drying out faster than the insides. Many home cheesemakers heat using a double boiler method by putting the cheese pot in a sink full of warm water and allowing the curds to gently heat, replacing it with warmer water as the stirring continues. I use the coolest edge of my wood cooking stove, keeping a careful eye on the temperature and alternating between the bench and the stove if I need to slow it down. Cheesemakers with gas or electric stoves can achieve gentle heating on the stovetop by switching a hotplate or burner on and off periodically, to allow some heat to get to the curds, but not heating too rapidly. The double boiler method is the most reliable one to ensure gentle heat.

You don't need to stand there the entire time stirring, but it's good to be around in the kitchen during the stirring stage, and to stir as often as you can, especially if the cheese is being heated, because you don't want the curds at the bottom of the pot to overheat, and leaving the curds alone for too long without stirring will result in the curds clumping together and not expelling as much whey as they should, or of some curds expelling more whey than others.

Stirring around once every five minutes works reasonably well.

Stir as gently as possible. Vigorous stirring causes whey to be released too quickly, so that you end up with a dry cheese, and sometimes fats will break down prematurely to give unwanted flavours to the cheese. In general, stir only just enough to stop your curds lumping together or sticking to the bottom of the pot.

If your curds do start getting stuck, use your hands to gently stir them while gently breaking them apart, trying to break them along the existing fracture lines rather than creating new ones.

Most hard cheeses are stirred until the curds begin to feel slightly springy when pressed and will hold together when a clump of them is squeezed. You can learn this process through feeling the texture of the fragile curds when they're first cut, and then feeling throughout the stirring process. At some point the curds will strengthen, and for many cheese recipes this is the time when they're ready to be put in the mould.

Another trick to tell when to finish stirring a hard cheese is to gather a small amount of curd in a flat hand, then close your hands together as if you are clapping. Tilt your hands up, so that the one the curd started on is now on top, and then open your hands – when the curd is ready, it will stick to the top hand (sometimes quite briefly, sometimes for longer) before falling down. If it sticks only briefly, you can decide whether to stop stirring now and continue with the cheese recipe, for a cheese with more moisture and a softer texture that will press more easily under less weight, or continue stirring, for the cheese to develop its maximum flavour and a firmer texture. Sometimes it will just take an extra five minutes of stirring to get to a much firmer curd.

Above, whisk-cut curds after 30 minutes heating and stirring. Curds are firmer and more whey has been lost.

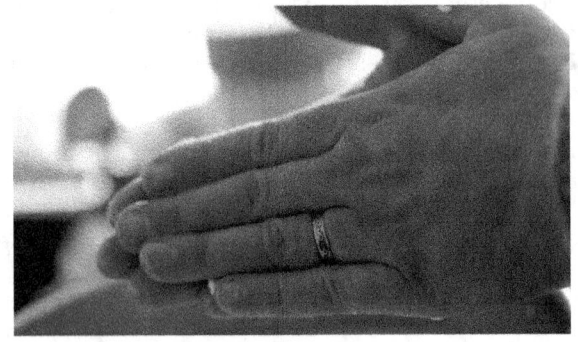

Above, stage 1 of the readiness test - getting a handful of curd. Below, stage 2 of the readiness text - squashing the handful of curds flat between two hands.

Above, whisk-cut curd texture 15 minutes after cutting - curds are delicate and soft. Not much whey has been lost.

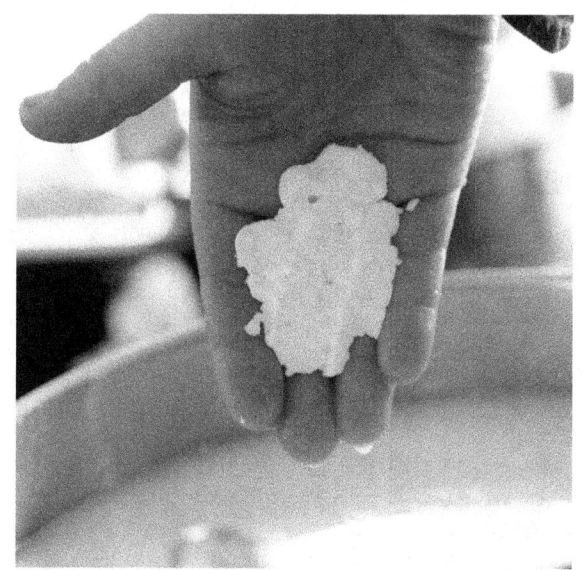

Above, stage 3 of the readiness test. Curds clump together and remain on my hand. This means they're ready for pressing.

Washing the curds

Some cheeses such as Havarti and Gouda have an additional step of washing the curds with warm water. This stage happens during the stirring process.

This technique was first developed by cheesemakers who used wooden vats to make their cheeses – the vats could not be directly heated, so the curds were encouraged to shrink by removing whey and replacing the whey with hot water. Some cheesemakers today use heated water as the sole heat source for these cheeses, and other cheesemakers use a combination of stove heat and hot water to bring the cheese to the correct temperature.

Washing the curds with either cold or warm water removes some of the lactose, leaving less lactose for the cultures to acidify, and more calcium in the cheese. This method gives the cheese a mild taste and pliable texture. With hot water cheeses such as Havarti and Gouda, this is done by removing a set amount of whey, and replacing it with the same amount of water during the curd stirring process.

There are some cheeses such as Colby and Monterey Jack which are instead washed with cool water after the curds have been stirred. This cool water process allows the curds to swell with more moisture, to create a kind of moister, milder alternative to Cheddar.

Other washed curd cheeses such as St Paulin and some versions of Havarti are washed with water the same temperature as the milk shortly after the curds are cut, with the goal temperature being reached with stove heat only, to reach similar temperatures and textures to the hot water Gouda and Havarti.

Washing the curds can be done to any cheese as an emergency measure. If you've left your cheese culturing or rennetting for too long and you suspect that too much acidity has been building up, you can use a washed curd technique to reduce the acidity of the whey and remove some of the remaining lactose.

Depending on how much acid has built up during the earlier stage of cheesemaking, somewhere between one quarter and one half of the whey is removed from the pot and replaced with water during the washing process.

Cheddaring

This is only done for Cheddar-style cheeses. Real cheddaring involves draining the whey, allowing the curds to clump together, cutting the curds into slabs and resting the slabs on top of each other to begin pressing the cheese while it's still developing acidity. The slabs are moved and restacked often to release as much whey as possible and firm up as they are pressed under their own weight.

Draining the whey

In warm weather, when the stirring has been completed and the curds have reached the right texture, curds are allowed to settle to the bottom of the pot (this usually takes around five minutes), and most of the whey is then carefully poured off. The curds are then gently placed into cheesecloth or cheese form to allow the rest of the whey to drain. Some cheeses are salted at this stage, but most cheeses rely on the salting of the rind during the aging process.

To drain soft cheeses such as chèvre and yoghurt cheese, the curd is first drained in a cheesecloth over a colander, and then the corners of the cheesecloth are tied together over a wooden spoon. The wooden spoon is suspended over a deep pot or bowl with enough room for whey to gather in the pot without touching the curds.

For hard cheeses, and cheeses set in moulds, the cheese is drained in a cheese hoop or cheese basket (often lined with cheesecloth) for the whey to drain while the cheese settles or is pressed into the preferred shape.

If you're making a small batch hard cheese in cold weather, it's important to be very quick in the draining process, as you do not want the curds to cool down too much before the pressing process begins. I do not first pre-drain the whey, but instead put my cheesecloth in the cheese mould, and place it inside a large bowl to catch the whey as it is poured. I carefully pour the curds and whey into the lined mould, to surround the curds with warm whey while I arrange the cheesecloth and get everything ready for pressing. This ensures that the curds are as warm as they possibly can be when they begin pressing.

The optimum temperature for draining cheeses is around 22°C (72°F).

Below 10°C (50°F) the acid development and release of whey is slowed (and sometimes stopped). If the temperature drops this low during draining, you may need to get the temperature higher again and then drain for longer. In higher temperatures, the draining is more rapid, sometimes too rapid for good chèvre, if you are draining cheese in weather warmer than 22°C, try to find a cooler place to drain your cheese, time your cheesemaking so that the draining happens at night or a cooler part of the day, and/or put ice bricks and jars of cold water near your cheese to reduce the temperature around it.

Shaping and pressing

During this stage, the cheese curds are placed in a form that will allow the rest of the whey to drain away. This can be cheesecloth over a colander, in the case of soft cheeses, or it can be a cheese hoop or basket with a follower, sometimes with weights or a press to press on it, as is used for hard cheeses. The cheese mould is lined carefully with cheesecloth, avoiding bunching up, the curds are then added and evenly arranged so that they're relatively flat on the surface, and the remainder of the cloth is carefully arranged in a way as to not leave big dents in the curd. I fold the edges of my cheesecloth over the top one edge at a time, carefully folding it when it reaches the next edge to avoid lumps.

For hard cheeses, I usually use an 800g cheese mould. This mould is 12cm (4 and 3/4 inches) in diameter, and 13.5cm (5 and 1/4 inches) high. This size mould works well for cheeses made from between three and eight litres (one to two gallons) of milk, and in summer if the milk is very low in solids, it has worked for ten litres (quarts) of goats milk.

Weights are added for pressed cheeses. If not much weight is needed, then canning jars filled with water can be a good option.

A cheese press is recommended for some hard cheeses. These come in a variety of styles, but generally all of them are using pressure generated through springs and similar devices to press down the follower on top of the cheese hoop to expel more whey. A cheese press that goes up to fifty pounds (twenty two kilograms) of weight, with the ability to use half of this amount of weight when needed is a good option for the home cheesemaker. It's not something you need right away, and many cheesemakers happily live without one.

In general, the drier the curd, the more pressure is needed. Salted curd cheeses such as Cheddar need a lot of pressure, most other cheeses can be pressed with jars of water and other small weights.

During the pressing phrase, it's a good idea to try and keep the curds at a warm room temperature of around 22°C (72°F). This keeps the cheese at the correct temperature for more acid development, and also encourages the curds to lose whey. Surrounding the mould with bottles of warm water, and even using warm water in a jar to press the cheese can also help to keep it warm in cold weather. If your kitchen is above 24°C (75°F) and you are making cows milk cheese there is some risk of the butterfat melting and running away with the whey. Pressing the cheese in a cooler part of the house, or surrounding the cheese with cool bottles of water might help. Using less pressure in warm weather can also be a good idea.

When first pressing the cheese, observe the colour of the whey coming out. If it's white and greasy then too much pressure is being applied.

Generally when a cheese is pressed, it will first be pressed with a smaller amount of weight, then the cheese will be removed from the press, flipped over and pressed with a higher amount of weight.

One of the goals of pressing cheese is to continue growing the acidity of the cheese while it presses. The next stage of salting will halt the acid production. If the cheese you are making is one that should melt, you can test whether it's ready to go on to the next stage by heating a piece of iron or stainless steel on the stove until hot, and then touching it to a small spot on the edge of your wheel – if your cheese is meant to melt, and is at the correct acidity for melting, the piece you are touching will start to melt and this will mean that it's ready to salt.

If you've been pressing your cheese at around 22°C (72°F) then it should all go according to the timing of the recipe; if the temperature dropped during the pressing time, you may need to press for longer, or if the pressing was done at a higher temperature, the cheese may have developed the right amount of acidity earlier than expected.

Above, curds in cheese mould, surrounded by a bowl of whey to keep them warm while I arrange the cloth.

Below, carefully folding the excess cloth on top of the curds. Lumps of cloth will leave indents in your cheese, so it's best to fold it as flat as possible, one side at a time.

Cheese pressing with a jar of water

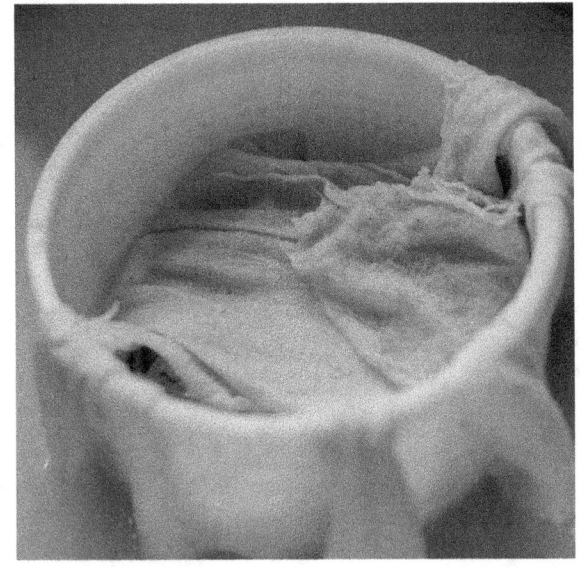

Above, flipping mould upside down after the first pressing.

Below, flipping the cheese over, so that the top side of the cheese from the last pressing is now at the bottom of the cheesecloth for the next pressing.

Above, carefully wrapping the sides of the cheese back in the cheesecloth to help prevent it from bunching up too much in any one place.

Below, putting the cheese back in the mould for the second pressing.

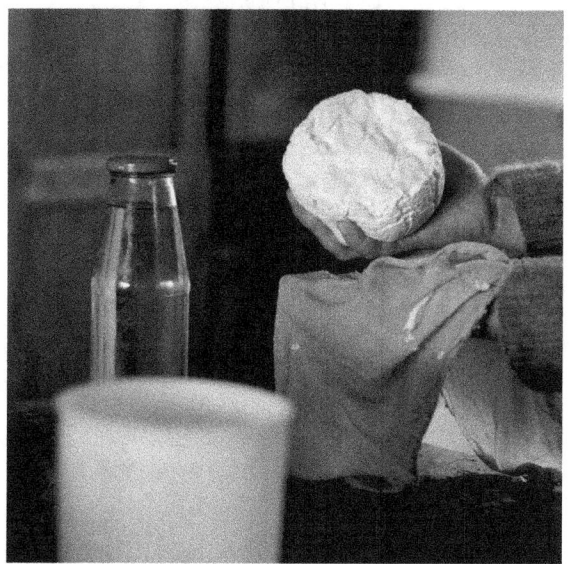

Salting

Salt is added to cheeses to halt the development of acid, to draw whey out of the curds, to discourage certain types of bacteria from growing on the cheese surface, while bringing out the flavour of the cheese.

The time to use salt in cheesemaking will depend on what style you're making. For fresh cheeses it is often mixed though the draining or freshly drained curd; for most hard cheeses it can be rubbed on the cheese after it has been pressed.

Larger-scale cheesemakers will often soak cheeses in a salty brine rather than directly salting the surface, but I think on a home-scale it is much easier to just use salt.

The type of salt to use is very important. It should be a pure salt with no additives such as iodine or anti-caking agent. Recommended salts for cheesemaking are Himalayan salt, Celtic sea salt, and any good sea salt without additives (keep in mind that some sea salts are refined and therefore saltier than others, so you may need to adjust the amount of salt in the recipe depending on what type you are using). Your salt will need to be finely ground. If in doubt, crush your salt with a pestle and mortar to make the grain of it finer.

The amount of unrefined salt to use when salting the surface of most hard cheeses is roughly one tablespoon (10g) for every one gallon (four litres) of milk used in the recipe. Reduce this amount by a quarter if you're using refined salt. Be observant of the seasonal conditions of the milk – if it is at a time of year when the cheese yield is low, reduce the amount of salt used, if you are making cheese with very thick milk, you may need to increase the amount of salt.

For more accuracy, you can weigh your pressed hard cheese, and then add the correct amount of unrefined salt for the weight of cheese, roughly 2.5% - 3.75% unrefined salt for most cheeses. This works out to be 5.5g to 7.5g (1.65 to 2.25 teaspoons) unrefined salt to 200g (7oz) cheese. Halve these amounts for Alpine cheese. Add a bit extra if you are aiming for Parmesan and Pecorino levels of salt.

For bloomy rind cheeses and aged chèvre, around 2.5% unrefined salt is ideal, or 5g (1 1/2 teaspoons) salt for 200g (7oz) cheese.

The above volumes and percentages are for using unrefined salt such as Himalayan salt. If you are using a refined salt such as a generic sea salt, reduce these amounts by ¼, for example, the average hard cheese would use around 5g (1 ½ teaspoons) refined salt for every 200g (7oz) of cheese.

For soft cheeses, adjust the salt to your taste, keeping in mind that it will become saltier as it drains, and that you can always add more later on if you need to. 1 tablespoon (15ml/10g) of unrefined salt for every gallon (four litres) of milk is usually around the right amount for milk with decent amounts of solids – use less salt if your milk is low in solids.

Ashing

Cheeses can have a coat of edible charcoal sprinkled over them, to form a contrast between the white inside and the charcoal layer, to add a subtle nutty flavour to the cheese, and to change the acidity of the cheese surface to encourage the bloomy white rinds to grow.

The charcoal is sometimes called ash and is generally added to the cheese when it has almost finished drying in an airy place, so that it doesn't have drips of whey coming out of it any more, but there is still some moisture on the surface for the ash to adhere to.

Ash can also be sprinkled in the middle of cheeses. This was generally done when there wasn't much milk, so the first half of the cheese was made on one day, sprinkled with ash to stop it forming a rind or getting bugs on it, and then the second half of the cheese was made the next day and put on top of this before the cheese was pressed. This method could be a way for backyard goatherds to make larger cheeses when there is only a small amount of milk available every day.

Fresh chèvre can be formed into a log, rolled in charcoal, and then eaten as-is. Aged chèvres such as Valençay are often treated in the same way, to form a charcoal stripe in between the bloomy white rind and the cheese inside. Ashed Brie is another well-known ashed cheese where the charcoal adds an extra dimension of flavour that enhances an already great cheese.

Cheesemaking ash can be made at home, by selecting oak or apple tree twigs (or other non-poisonous twigs), or grape vines, keeping them all around the same size, and putting them inside a tin can with a lid or wrapping them in foil, punching a hole in the lid or package for air to escape, and then putting it on a fire until smoke comes out of the hole. The length of time this will take will depend on the size of the twigs. In an oven, charcoal can be made from vegetables such as leeks and onions by just overcooking them so much that they turn to charcoal. Once the charcoal is made it can be crushed in a mortar and pestle and used on your cheeses. Charcoal for cheeses can also be bought from cheesemaking supply shops, where it's generally known as 'vegetable ash'.

Adding herbs and spices

Herbs and spices can either be mixed through the curds before pressing, pressed cheeses can be rolled in a layer of them before aging, or you can mix ground herbs or spices with olive oil, and use this mixture to rub the rind of your cheese during the aging process.

If you're adding spices or herbs directly to the curds, it's best to boil them in water first, to help avoid contamination and to soften them if they're dried. Once they're boiled, the infused water can be mixed into the cultured milk before adding the rennet, and the whole spices are mixed through the curds after the whey has been drained off, so that they don't float away with the whey.

The trick with adding any spice or herb directly to the cheese curds is not to overwhelm the natural flavour of the cheese, but to complement it. If in doubt, experiment by using a small amount of the spice, and then taste to see whether you would prefer it with more added or with less. Usually somewhere between a quarter of a teaspoon and one and a half teaspoons per gallon (4 litres) of milk is a good amount to add.

Caraway is often added to cheeses such as Gouda

and Havarti, and if you love the taste of caraway, it will definitely be appreciated in milder cheeses such as these. Use ¼ to ½ teaspoon per gallon (4 litres) of milk, as the flavour can be quite strong.

Cumin can be used in a similar way to caraway, but adds a different taste.

Peppercorns and Tasmanian mountain pepperberries can also be used in cheeses. These are added at higher amounts, up to one teaspoon per gallon of milk.

Red pepper flakes (chilli flakes) can be added to cheeses, to give heat, flavour, and colour. Add these to the curds before pressing, as you would for caraway, or rub onto the outside of the cheese with olive oil during aging.

Some cheeses are traditionally wrapped in a layer of fresh herb leaves such as nettle or wild garlic, before being aged.

Other cheeses are sometimes rubbed with a mix of olive oil and dried spices (such as smoked paprika).

Fresh or dried herbs and spices can also be mixed through soft cheeses such as chèvre and ricotta, to add different flavours. This is especially appreciated if you want to make a soft cheese using the simple jar method I use for chèvre (page 78), but using a mild cows milk – the herbs or spices will make for a more interesting cheese.

Alcohol can be used as a final wash for the curds to add more unique flavours. To do this, make any cheese and drain all whey off to get it ready to press, put the curds back in the pot, and then add a decent splash of your choice of beer, wine, or whiskey, mixing it through with your hands and allowing it to soak for five to ten minutes, before putting the curds in the mould ready for pressing.

Airing

Most cheeses are aired to evaporate any excess moisture and to begin developing a rind before they are moved to the cheese cave. The space for doing this should essentially be open to fresh air, but constructed in a way to stop insects landing on the cheese. You can do this directly in the cheese cave if it's completely free of insects. The temperature for this doesn't have to be quite as cold or stable as the cheese cave, but it is best to keep it as low as possible, so try to keep it away from the cooking stove, the sun, and other sources of heat.

The ideal temperature is 15°C (59°F). As low as 12°C (53°F) and up to 18°C (64°F) is fine. Higher temperatures will mean faster drying, lower temperatures will slow it down.

Some old cupboards have sections with fly screen on the sides that work really well for this. The type of meat safe made from fly screen or metal punched with holes, placed in a draughty place where it's not too warm will also do the job well. Fly-proof food covers, constructed as wire hoops covered with fly screen will also work. If there aren't any flies or mice around you can just air the cheese out in the open.

While the cheese is being aired, it's important to flip it at least twice every day, moving to a dry bit of surface each time, to help evenly dry both sides of the cheese.

The airing process usually takes 24 to 48 hours - more airing will lead to a drier rind, less airing will mean more whey leaking over your cheese aging shelves.

Aging cheeses

The aging time for a cheese will depend on the recipe. Soft cheeses are best used right away. Feta and halloumi need at least a few days in salt or brine before they're ready. Camembert and some other soft surface-ripened cheeses need four to six weeks. Hard cheeses generally need three weeks or more before they're ready to eat, and for some of them, if they're kept in the right conditions, their flavour will be better if they're left for longer. Some hard cheeses such as vintage Cheddar and Parmesan are aged for eighteen months to two years. The optimum aging time for each cheese will depend on the conditions they are kept in, how active the cultures are, the size of the cheese, and the style of cheese that you're trying to make.

In general, smaller batch cheeses will be ready earlier than larger ones, so a six litre (six quart) batch of tomme will be delicious after one month, and after two months will have a similar depth of flavour to a six month aged twenty litre (five gallon) batch.

If aged much longer than three months, a small batch cheese can begin to dry out more, creating more of a Parmesan-style cheese that is perfect for grating and serving with meals, or serving in thin slivers on its own. To slow this process to keep your cheese softer for longer, the aged cheese can be stored as-is in a bucket of wood ash, wrapped in parchment baking paper and either left on the shelf, or put in the fridge or freezer.

Cheeses should not be packed in close together when they're being aged. There should be space around each cheese to allow for airflow.

During the first week of aging, cheeses need to be flipped over and moved to a dry surface once every day or two. After the first week, cheeses need to be flipped over around once a week, and the rinds of some cheeses will need to be carefully rubbed or brushed, to discourage unwanted fungus and encourage a rind to form. You can also add extra salt to the rind at this stage, especially if the "cat hair" fungus is growing on your cheese (this is a harmless fungus that signifies that the cheese hasn't had enough salt - it is a fluffy grey fungus that grows to look a bit like clumps of cat hair). To get rid of it, rub salt on the places where you see it (or over the whole cheese).

The best surface for a cheese to age on is untreated wood, but specialist plastic cheese aging mats also do the job. Sushi mats can also be used. Try to move your cheese to a dry area of the aging surface every time you check on it, this helps avoid the buildup of unwanted fungus.

In general, cheeses are best aged at around 55°F (13°C). For cheeses sealed in wax, the humidity doesn't matter, but for natural rind cheeses, it's best if the humidity is generally around seventy to eighty percent. Traditionally, underground caves would provide the optimum environment for aging cheeses. For the home cheesemaker a number of options are available, which I will discuss below.

The ideal cheese aging space

The reason why we often refer to the aging space as a cheese cave is because caves provide the ideal conditions of low and stable temperature, high humidity, and some ventilation. You can make aged cheeses without perfect conditions, and I will discuss this below, but to begin with, if we first look at a traditional cheese cave, we can learn what it is that makes cheeses age so well in caves, and find ways to get these conditions at home

The ideal cheese cave has a stable temperature, with not much variation beyond 3°C of a particular temperature, for example, the average temperature in the aging space might be 10°C (50°F), sometimes dropping to 7°C (44.5°F) overnight and rising to 13°C (55.5°F) sometimes during the day. The more stable the temperature is, the better the aging space. Low temperature fluctuations are achieved with thermal mass – a traditional root cellar uses the stable thermal mass of the earth to buffer against fluctuations, my own not-so-perfect larder has a tiled floor, cement walls, and a bunch of full canning and fermenting jars keeping the temperature reasonably stable.

Fairly low temperature is ideal, but too low will halt the aging process. Between 8°C (46°F) and 15°C (59°F) is best. Lower temperatures mean slower aging (and often more mould growth) higher temperatures mean faster aging and often less mould.

To encourage low temperatures, vents or windows into your aging space can be opened at night or in times of cold temperature and closed when the outside temperatures are too high. There are also electrical gadgets such as coolbots that can help cool the cheese aging space.

High humidity is good to have when working with natural rinds, as this allows the cheeses to age without drying out the rinds too much, and encourages moulds which help to age the cheese. Caves are naturally high in humidity. To increase the humidity in your aging space, you can hang a wet towel from a rail, with the bottom of it in a tray of water. The towel will wick water upwards, adding to the humidity in the air.

If your humidity is less than ideal, there are a few options:
• Being happy with what nature provides. In the dry times of the year, rinds will be drier and cheeses more Parmesan-like. In wetter times of the year you will have more moulds and softer cheeses.
• Waxing, oiling, clothbinding, or leaf wrapping the cheeses.
• Making cheeses with higher moisture content to begin with, such as the washed curd cheeses. These are less likely to crack in low humidity.
• Adding more humidity, as with wet towels and trays of water in the aging space.
• Using closed containers with small vents for some of the cheese aging. These containers restrict airflow and allow the moisture in the cheese to humidify the air around itself. These need to be watched carefully as they can sometimes restrict too much airflow.

Our ancestors did not have humidity monitors, and aged their cheeses with experience, observation, seasonal variation, and some guesswork. We can do the same.

Ventilation is necessary for cheese aging. Cheeses breathe as they age, and if they don't have enough fresh air to breathe then ammonia smells and nasty tastes can develop. Too much ventilation usually means lower humidity, so you don't want to go overboard with it, but having a window open at certain times, a vent, or opening the door every day, depending on your aging space, will help with ventilation.

Cheeses also need space around them. For the first week or so of aging, the surface underneath the cheese will be damp, and the cheese needs to be moved onto a dry surface. During the whole aging process, the cheeses should not be packed close together, but allowed some space for air to circulate. At a bare minimum, allow an inch or two between cheeses in shelf width, plus twice the width of each cheese in shelf depth (or extra shelf width, if using shallow shelves), to allow for dry space to flip the cheese onto.

For the height between shelves, more height is better than less. Ideally allow around four times the height of each cheese in between shelves for air to circulate. The more cheeses you are making and the smaller the space you are working with, the more important this is. Cheeses need to breathe!

Passive cheese cave or root cellar

For anyone serious about cheesemaking who doesn't intend to move house any time soon, there is the option of constructing a cave in your own yard. This could be an aboveground cave, made from straw bales or cob, or the traditional underground, or partly underground root cellar, often set into the side of a hill. To have the humidity that cheese aging needs, it's best for it to have an earth floor. If you're planning on aging a lot of cheese at once, it's a good idea to have a vent towards the top of the cave, to allow gases from the cheese aging process to easily escape without heating up the cave. If the door is very airtight it's worthwhile to also have a small vent low down on the door or wall to draw some fresh air into the cave.

Traditional larders and cool cupboards, more passive options

A traditional larder is based on a combination of thermal mass (where possible), along with avoiding adding heat, and some airflow. An unheated room in the house with a window that doesn't get much direct sunlight can be used, especially if the window can be screened against insects and opened often.

The ideal traditional larder would have a screened window that never gets any direct sun, thermal mass would be from the floor being in contact with the earth (perhaps also from cob or mudbrick walls). My larder is far from this ideal, as my home is on pole foundations and the window gets some sun in summer, but it still is definitely possible to age many lovely cheeses in this room.

I use a room in my house for a larder where we get direct sunlight sometimes on summer afternoons. The cool nighttime temperatures here allow us to open the window and bring cool air into the room, which then cools down the thermal mass of the tiled floor and cement walls. In our larder, it gets hotter than ideal at times on summer days, and sometimes the cheeses leak some fat if there's a heatwave, but for the most part I've found that having a larder where the temperature is usually between 8°C (46°F) and 15°C (59°F), sometimes at 20°C (68°F) briefly, and sometimes even a little higher than that for short times is fine for aging most cheeses.

If you're not sure if a room in the house will make a good larder or not, open the window as much as possible, put a jar of water in the room with your cheese thermometer in it and observe the temperature a few times during the day.

To quickly add thermal mass into an existing room, if your floor isn't on slab or earth foundations, you can increase the thermal mass of it by covering it in bricks or tiles (just make sure the floor can handle the extra weight first!). More thermal mass can be added in the form of large containers of water, filled canning jars, or more bricks. If your window gets some direct sunlight, awnings can be added outside the window to block high summer sun, or shady trees and vines planted in front of it to block morning or afternoon sun.

A "cold cupboard" or "cool cupboard" is something that can be built into a new home or retrofitted into existing homes as an alternative to a fridge, or as a dedicated cheese aging cupboard. These are cupboards with a vent at the base that brings cold air from under the house up into the cupboard, with a small chimney at the top, usually painted black to draw heat upwards in order to keep the cupboard cool. Thick doors help avoid heat getting into the cupboard. David Holmgren's book Retrosuburbia has some details on this. Searching online for "cool cupboard" will find other useful information.

To help keep the humidity high in a cool cupboard, make sure that the vents can be closed if needed, in case the airflow ends up drying out the cheeses too much.

Seasonal cheese aging

For the home cheesemaker in a temperate or cold climate who doesn't want electrical gadgets and can't build an outdoor cheese cave or indoor cold cupboard, finding a place in the house that is consistently at the right cheese aging temperature for at least one month of the year and making hard cheeses during that time is the best option.

Most successful for us has been an unheated room with an open window that doesn't get direct sunlight, as discussed in the section about traditional larders. In the past we have also successfully used an old fridge, switched off, on a shady porch. Crawlspaces under the house can work as well, as long as there are not large amounts of radon gas there, and as long as the cheese is on a side that doesn't get much direct sun (east, or either north in the northern hemisphere, or south in the southern hemisphere), if you're using a crawlspace, the cheese will need to be kept in something that is rodent-proof, such as an old metal meat safe.

With seasonal cheese aging, aged cheeses are usually made in autumn and winter, when the temperature and humidity are right for aging. Observe your space throughout the year, and notice if the temperature changes much on hot days; you may find that you can age cheese at any time of the year this way.

Old-fashioned metal meat safe hanging outdoors. The many small holes punched into the metal allow for airflow.

Wine fridges, and other modified thermostat fridges

An electrical option for anyone that has trouble finding the right conditions for cheese aging is to use a wine fridge set at cheese aging temperature (usually the red wine setting is perfect for cheese), or a regular fridge with a thermostat gadget added to it to keep it at a higher temperature than the standard fridge temperature. If using a fridge with a modified thermostat, for best results try to find one without a freezer compartment. If your fridge has glass shelves, remove them and replace them with wood or slatted shelves of some sort, as glass shelves can drip condensation onto the cheeses below. If you're using any kind of fridge, it's important to open and close the door each day to give your cheeses some fresh air.

Humidity is usually on the low side in fridges of all kinds, and can be increased to ideal cheese aging humidity by adding a wet towel to the bottom of the fridge and wetting it again every now and then, as needed. A 'Coolgardie safe' inspired system can also be implemented, by having a pan of water at the bottom of the fridge, and a towel draping into it from a shelf to wick water up and add more humidity to the air.

Working with moulds during the aging process

Aging natural cheeses is a natural process, and for the best experience it can help to let go of expectations, try not to control things too much, and just appreciate what you do create. I like to think of this approach as a permaculture approach – working with nature.

If you would like to help a particular cheese along to develop the results you would like, there are ways to do this naturally.

If you prefer cheeses without much mould, having more ventilation in your aging space, less humidity, and flipping and moving your cheeses often to a dry breathable surface (such as wood) will help reduce mould growth. During the first couple of weeks of aging, the cheeses can be moved once or twice a day to a dry surface, flipping each time, and this will help to avoid mould development. Rubbing the surfaces of your cheeses with a dry cloth, or a little extra salt can help to curb mould growth, as will wiping with a cloth dipped in vinegar.

If your cheeses are not getting as much mould growth as you would like, it's possible to find ways to increase the humidity. One method is to have a plastic box, either with a vent in the lid and an elevated rack inside, or with a normal lid left ajar. Leave the vent open, to help give a small amount of ventilation. Keep the cheese off the base of the box with some kind of rack or block of wood. If you want to avoid plastic directly on the cheese surface, you can usually tuck a sushi mat or small piece of wood inside these boxes for the cheese to sit on.

The most crucial time for developing moulds is the first couple of weeks, so there's no need to keep the cheese in the box the whole aging time, just move it onto another aging surface once it's developed some mould, or in the case of bloomy white cheeses such as Brie and Camembert, move them from the box and then wrap them in some beeswax wrap, parchment baking paper, or cheese wrap to continue aging with high humidity.

Moulds can be encouraged by wiping your cheese every day or two for the first week using a cloth dipped in salted whey. If you can add a small piece of your favourite mouldy cheese rind to this whey and leave it to soak overnight, this will make the process faster and more reliable. For best results, also increase the humidity by having your cheese in an enclosed box for the first week or two, as described above.

Coating a cheese's surface with vegetable ash (edible charcoal) will also encourage white moulds to develop, see page 57 for details.

Often with white rind cheeses made without packet ingredients, it is the wrinkly white geotrichum candidum mould which is dominant rather than the fluffy penicillium candidum mould that we're more familiar with. They have a similar taste and work in the same way, so don't be alarmed if your white mould cheese looks wrinkly – this is actually very good!

With natural cheeses made from raw milk, moulds other than the intended white moulds often develop. I don't worry if my Camembert ends up speckled with blue. One Camembert I made had a succession of moulds starting with pure white to begin with, followed by a few blue speckles, and ending up pure blue at the end of aging – this still tasted like a Camembert even though it looked like a blue cheese. Most of my bloomy white cheeses don't get that far, usually they just have blue speckles as well as white moulds, and we enjoy them all the same.

One of the white moulds we see on natural cheeses actually starts out white and then turns blue – it's still the same mould, just a different colour. Moulds often work in succession, with the white moulds being first to colonise the surfaces, changing the conditions of the surface to then allow other moulds to grow. If you want to try and slow the mould development as soon as the white mould has developed, reduce the humidity for hard cheeses, or for soft cheeses, wrap the cheese and reduce the temperature to fridge-like temperatures for the rest of aging.

If you want to have a stinky orange rind on your cheese, just keep on wiping the rind of your cheese with a cloth dipped in salted whey or ale every day until the orange mould develops. If you can include some stinky orange cheese rind in your salted whey, this will definitely help it along.

Waxed rinds, clothbound rinds, and oiled rinds

Waxed rinds and clothbound rinds can be an option if you want no mould at all. One issue with waxed and clothbound rinds is that you can't see what is going on under the surface. Moulds can develop sometimes, and because you can't see them, you can't control them by rubbing or salting as you would with natural rinds.

For success with waxed rinds, get your cheese to just the right state of dryness before covering it in a couple of layers of hot melted beeswax by salting the cheese and allowing it to dry out in a place with a dry surface and plenty of airflow for five to seven days, flipping and moving the cheese twice a day to a fresh dry surface so that it can dry as quickly as possible. This is the hardest part of making waxed cheeses, as it can be difficult to find the ideal stage where the cheese has dried out enough that it's not going to have too much moisture under the wax, but is not aged so much that it's already started developing moulds. Observe carefully, and wax your cheese as soon as you notice that there's no moisture left on the surface when you flip it.

To wax a cheese, first carefully heat your wax using

the double boiler method (it is highly flammable). 93°C (200°F) is ideal for killing any mould spores on the surface of the cheese, but can also be dangerous, so lower temperatures can also be used. You can either dip your cheese into the pot of wax, one side first, waiting for that side to dry before waxing the other side, or you can use a pastry brush to brush the wax onto your cheese. Do at least two coats of wax on all sides for best results.

For a clothbound rind, just follow any cheese recipe, salt the cheese, leave to air for a day or two, and then follow the clothbinding instructions from the Cheddar recipe on page 114. A clothbound cheese will end up with a different taste to the same cheese made with a waxed rind, as the cheese can still breathe and dry out more as it ages, and when mould develops on a clothbound cheese, it's often a small amount of blue or white.

Oiling your cheese can discourage moulds and cheese mites. Olive oil is traditionally used on Parmesan-type cheeses, and can be used on any cheese. To oil a cheese, first wait for a week or two, until the rind has dried. If there are any moulds, brush them off first, and then rub oil onto the rind. One coat can be enough, or feel free to add more coats of oil if the rind is looking very dry, or if you have any more unwanted moulds appearing.

Spices of your choice can be added to the oil and rubbed in at the same time, smoked paprika being a popular choice from Spain. You can choose any spice that will complement your cheese – turmeric adds a subtle flavour and makes for a yellow-rinded cheese, red pepper will add heat and flavour, crushed caraway or black pepper will add classic flavours that go with any cheese, and cacao powder can be used for a striking brown-rinded cheese, either with spices or on its own. You can be as creative as you like with adding spices to the rinds in this way The spices also help to further discourage moulds, as well as adding different tastes to the cheese.

Leaf wrapping

Another way to change the rind of your cheese is to wrap it in non-toxic leaves, either using fresh leaves, frozen leaves, boiled leaves, or leaves that have been soaked in whiskey, brandy, or other alcohol for at least a week. Traditional choices include nettle, maple, chestnut, grape, and walnut, but any non-poisonous leaves can be used.

As well as preventing the rind from drying out too much, fresh leaves encourage different bacteria on the surface of the cheese, and alcohol-soaked leaves introduce the flavour of the alcohol to the rind of the cheese without adding any additional bacteria.

To leaf wrap any hard cheese, first allow it to develop a rind, as you would for waxing, and then wrap it completely in leaves, securing the leaves with string. For bloomy rinds, allow them to develop some white bloom first before wrapping.

It is far easier to just use one leaf, and work with smaller cheeses, than it is to try and arrange several leaves over a larger cheese. Before shaping your cheese, observe the size of the leaf you intend to wrap it in and make sure your cheese can be completely covered.

Flip your wrapped cheese over once a week during aging.

For best results, choose young leaves that are thin and flexible, and remove the tough centre stem if there is one. Rinse the leaves first and allow the water to dry off before wrapping. If the leaves are not soft enough to be flexible, boil them briefly or freeze them until softened before wrapping.

For alcohol-soaked leaves, just put your leaves in a container, sprinkle with enough brandy or other alcohol to get them thoroughly coated, and leave them to marinate for a week or more, flipping over every so often to make sure all of the leaves get soaked.

The best time to make cheese

The best time to make hard cheese is naturally when you have lots of milk. If you have a limited amount of milk, you can arrange to have a cheesemaking day by not making any yoghurt, soft cheese or other dairy foods for a day or two, and limiting the amount of milk that's used for drinking. The length of time you can keep your milk for cheesemaking will depend on how cold you can keep it, how clean everything is, and how comfortable you feel with using older milk.

These days I prefer to use milk that is as fresh as possible, so I will save the previous day's milk for drinking, and start on the cheese as soon after milking as I can, using a whole morning's milking.

Unless you don't have many responsibilities beyond cheesemaking, it's best to plan to be doing indoors chores or pottering around the kitchen when the cheese needs to be stirred. I like to plan to do my non-kitchen chores while the milk is culturing and setting into curds, and then to be either cooking food or doing a big wash up and kitchen clean while the curds need to be stirred.

Many cheesemaking books will tell you to stir the cheese non-stop for forty five minutes, but this is something I can't imagine many home cheesemakers doing in practise. If you don't stir the cheese often enough, the curds will begin to knit together, but stirring around every five minutes is fine, and if they do begin to knit together it is not such a big deal, as you can just gently break them apart again and make sure to tend them more frequently next time. Alternatively, if you don't have many responsibilities or noisy toddlers around on cheesemaking day you could always read with one hand while stirring with the other, or listen to music or watch videos.

Taking notes, record keeping, and improving your cheese skills

When I'm making a cheese, I will often note down the different times and temperatures of the cheese. I do this for the purpose of remembering what time I need to come back to the cheese to do the next step, and also to keep records in case I want to recreate a great cheese. The times I will note down are:

- Culture time and temperature.
- Rennet (temperature is usually the same or similar to the culturing one, so I only write that down if it's different).
- Curds cut (if I'm cutting with a whisk instead of a knife I will note that down). If the temperature has dropped significantly during rennetting I will note this down too.
- First press or draining start time and the temperature of the whey right before draining.
- Second press start time, and any additional pressings.

- The date that the cheese was made. Notes about weather conditions or biodynamic calendar days could be made too if needed.

How my notes look in real life for a cooked curd cheese might be are something like:
Culture 12pm 29°C
Rennet 1:10
Curds cut with whisk 1:30
First press 3:10 49°C water bottle
Second press 3:30 Fowlers jar
Third press cheese press

These notes help me while I'm making a cheese, as I won't always remember what time I started something, so by noting down the time of culturing, I know when to add rennet, and so on, and they also help improve cheesemaking skills over time, as I can go back to my notes and find out exactly how I made a cheese if I want to try and replicate it, and if coagulation is slower than expected or there are any other issues, I can work out ways to improve the next batch.

From the above cheese notes, I can see that I used the cheese press when I prefer not to for this style of cheese, I can also see that the culturing and stirring phases went for longer than ideal – I know from past experience that doing this will often result in curds that need more pressure.

With aged cheeses, these notes are backed up with a storage and labelling system for my cheeses. I have three shelves of my larder dedicated to cheeses, and I keep my cheeses organised on these shelves by date, so that the oldest cheeses are on the top right, and once the top shelf is full, the middle shelf starts filling up from the right as well. When one cheese gets eaten from the top, I move the rightmost cheese from the middle shelf up to the leftmost place of the top shelf, to keep my cheeses well organised. Having the oldest and driest cheeses on the top shelf means that there is no risk of new cheeses leaking whey onto the older cheeses.

To label individual cheeses, once it is ready for salting I use a butter knife to carefully carve out a small letter on one side of the cheese, so for tomme, I have "T", for alpine/cooked curd cheeses, I have "A". To carve these letters out, I first make an angled cut on one side of the line I'd like made, and then make another angled cut to remove a thin piece of cheese. This works out to be much easier to read than just writing on the cheese with a knife, which can fuse over. My method leaves a wider channel that is very obvious to read. Make sure to rub plenty of salt into the letter to avoid it becoming a place for excess mould to gather. Havarti is the cheese I make roughly half the time, it is eaten quite young and I don't bother labelling it – I just know that all the unlabeled ones are Havarti.

In the past I have carved the date onto the cheese in a similar manner, but this takes more time and leaves more dents in the cheese surface. A code could be used, so that a single letter, shape, or number could be carved, and then written down with the cheese notes for that particular cheese so that you can link up the cheese with the notes about making it and know exactly how old it is and how it was made.

To get more fancy about labelling individual cheeses, a plastic shape can be carved out of a yoghurt bucket lid or other food grade plastic and added to the top of the cheese before the cheesecloth is folded over and the weight added. As the cheese is pressed, the plastic shape will impress itself upon the surface of the cheese.

Another option for labeling individual cheeses is to give them a designated spot on the shelf, and then attach a label to that part of the shelf, either a label attached with string to a nail, or a bit of masking tape. Once the cheese is eaten, just remove the label and a different cheese can go there.

For anyone wanting the most detailed cheese records possible, a batch number or symbol can be noted on the cheese diary page, and then this can be used on the cheese label, so that it's very easy to match them both together and know the exact history of a particular cheese.

By taking these notes, we know how long the cheese has aged, so we know when the best time to start eating it is. Once we eat it, if it's exceptionally good, then we can go back and try to recreate these settings, or if there are some flaws, then we can look at the notes and sometimes spot what went wrong.

Notes and labelling are not an essential part of cheesemaking, and you can make great cheeses without them, but they can be a useful tool for helping to refine and grow your cheese skills.

How to Use Leftover Whey

When there is cheese, there is also whey. Many home cheesemakers see the whey as waste and tip it down the sink, but I prefer to think of whey as a resource. Whey contains varying amounts of protein, calcium, B vitamins, and other goodness ready to be used in the kitchen and around the homestead. Mostly I make gjetost when I can, and feed the other whey to my animals, but there are some other ways to use it which I'll share below.

The main thing to remember about using whey is that there are two different types: acid whey is from ricotta, paneer, quick mozzarella and anything else that is acidified with vinegar or other acids. If you need to use up this acidified whey, be careful that the method you use below says 'any kind of whey or just plain 'whey', as the methods that can only be used with cultured whey will not work with acid-curdled whey.

Cultured whey or live culture whey is from the cheeses in this book that are cultured with kefir or other cultures – it's milder and full of good bacteria, and can be used to culture more foods such as ferments and drinks. If the whey is from chèvre, quark, or another slowly cultured cheese, it will be more sour than whey from a hard cheese and can not be used for gjetost, but it is good for all other purposes.

To get the clearest whey, for a longer storage life and for use as as a starter culture for fermented vegetables and drinks, after allowing the whey to sit for at least an hour, skim the milky stuff off the top and strain the rest of the whey through cheesecloth to obtain the clearest whey.

Whey in the kitchen

• Use hard cheese whey, feta whey, halloumi whey, or slow mozzarella whey to make Gjetost (Norwegian whey cheese) (page 118).

• Use hard cheese whey, feta whey, halloumi whey, or slow mozzarella whey to make whey ricotta – just heat it up to around 88°C (190°F), not adding any acids, and delicate ricotta curds will form. Once you've skimmed out the ricotta curds, the rest of the whey can still be boiled down for Gjetost.

• Fresh live culture whey can be used as a cheese starter.

• Use whey with live cultures as a starter culture for sauerkraut, pickles and other fermented vegetables.

• Use whey with live cultures to preserve plums for several months by filling a jar with plums and topping up with whey to above the level of the plums.

• Make whey soda from whey with live cultures. Just use 60ml (1/4 cup) whey for every 1 litre (1 quart) of fruit juice or sweetened herbal tea and leave to ferment at room temperature until it's as sour as you like.

• Serve cultured whey as a drink on its own.

• Use any whey instead of water in cakes, muffins, breads, soups, and stocks. Reduce the amount of vinegar called for in any baking recipe, and if the recipe calls for baking powder, replace this with half the amount of bicarb soda (baking soda).

• Soak grains in whey overnight before cooking. Whey can also be used instead of water for cooking grains and pasta.

Whey for animals

• Use any kind of whey to soak grain overnight for pigs, chickens, and ducks to reduce the amount of other feed they eat. The whey provides extra protein and minerals, and the soaking helps increase the feed value of the grain, helping your animals to absorb more nutrients from it.

• Leave out a shallow pan of whey (any kind) for your pigs and poultry to drink instead of water. This strategy is not as reliable as soaking grains, as not all animals will drink whey on its own.

Whey in the garden

• Use whey with live cultures to water plants, to give them extra nutrition and anti-fungal properties. Just dilute the whey with water so that it's 1 part whey to 10 parts water.

• Any kind of whey can be added to the compost heap.

Cheese recipes

The cheeses that will work best in your home will depend on what milk you are using, what the animals were eating, the cheesemaking and maturing environment, how much time you have, and what you personally like to eat.

You may find yourself eating a lot more soft cheese than you previously did, because it's so easy to make and at its best when freshly made. If you have any cheesemaking failures along the way, the times when it does work will taste even better. Cheesemaking can be a complicated subject, yet to begin by making some simple fresh cheeses is really easy, so that is where the recipes will start.

Beyond that, the recipes up to a certain point go in order of difficulty: chèvre is extremely simple to learn and eat. Fast mozzarella is a great way to make a pizza cheese while learning about working with rennetted cheeses and watching the curds shrink as they are stirred. Feta is a simple aged cheese with less fussy aging requirements, teaching more skills along the way and creating a great cheese for eating fresh or using in salads and pies. Beyond this are the worlds of hard cheeses, blue cheeses, and surface-ripened cheese, slightly more complicated cheeses, but very easy to learn once you've had experience with the basics of making cultured and rennetted cheeses.

An important note about ingredients

Always use salt without any anti-caking agent, iodine, or other additives. For my recipes you will need a fine-grain salt, such as fine Himalayan salt or fine Celtic sea salt. If you can't find either of these unrefined salts you can use a refined fine salt such as flossy salt or dairy salt, or smash up some rock salt in a mortar and pestle. If you're using a refined salt, make sure to reduce the amount in these recipes by around $\frac{1}{4}$ to compensate for the increased saltiness.

For consistent results with rennetted cheeses please make sure that your rennet has been stored in a cool, dry environment and is not past its best before date. If you're not sure, you can test your rennet using the information on page 22 to see if it is working with your milk correctly.

I recommend natural animal rennet. This is usually from calves, but can be made at home as well. My next choice would be microbial rennet, which is vegetarian and not genetically modified.

I would personally avoid fermented chymosin rennet, as it is genetically modified, but if you choose to use this then the recipes in this book will still work as expected.

Always find out first how strong the rennet you are using is before you begin. You may find that the 'regular' dose of rennet to use changes depending on which brand you are using and seasonal milk changes throughout the year. Tomme, Parmesan, and the Alpine cheeses use a stronger dose of rennet than the regular dose, so once you find out the regular amount of rennet to use for Cheddar, Gouda, feta and so on, you can increase this amount to make the harder cheeses.

Ricotta and paneer
Simple acid and heat curdled cheeses

A good introduction to cheesemaking is by making a whole milk ricotta or paneer. These can be made with ingredients you already have in your kitchen, and are a good way to use up milk that's been sitting in the fridge longer than you'd like to drink it raw. Ricotta can be used in cheesecakes, savoury and sweet tarts, and also mixed with herbs and other flavourings to make dips or sandwich fillings. Paneer is ricotta that has been salted and pressed, to form a block of cheese that can be pan fried and then eaten by itself, used in curries, or in place of tofu in recipes.

A whole milk ricotta is basically milk that has been heated up to an almost-boiling temperature, and then the right amount of vinegar or lemon juice is stirred through and the mixture is left alone until it separates into curds and whey, then left to rest for around 15 minutes. The mixture is then strained through cloth, to separate the whey from the curds.

Paneer is often heated to higher temperatures than ricotta, or held at the high temperature for a period of time, to help develop a stronger protein structure for pressing.

Ingredients
2 litres (2 quarts) milk

60ml (¼ cup) cider vinegar or lemon juice, plus 2 tablespoons more if needed (or alternative, see note)

Optional ½ teaspoon salt

Equipment
Saucepan
Spoon
Cheesecloth
Colander

Method

1. Heat
Slowly heat the milk in a pot over a medium low heat, stirring every now and then to ensure the bottom doesn't scald, until it is very hot and almost boiling (it should reach a temperature of around 85°C (185°F) for ricotta, or 93°C (199°F) for paneer).

2. Add vinegar
Continue to stir and slowly pour in the vinegar while stirring for a few seconds more. Stop stirring, remove it from the heat, and leave it to rest - it should begin to separate into white curds and green or yellow whey within a minute. If the whey appears to still have a lot of milk

in it at this point, add a tablespoon or two more of vinegar while gently stirring.

3. Rest
Leave it to rest for 15 minutes.

4. Strain
Carefully arrange your cheesecloth to cover the colander, in one layer if you're using butter muslin or tight cheesecloth, or in four layers if you're using loosely-woven cheesecloth. When the curds and whey have rested for 15 minutes, carefully pour them or spoon them into the lined colander. Leave to drain for around 20 minutes. You now have ricotta.

5. Add optional salt
If you're adding salt to the ricotta, mix it through now. Use half a teaspoon of salt to two litres (two quarts) milk if you want to make paneer.

6. Making paneer
To make your salted ricotta into paneer: loosely fold the cheesecloth over the salted ricotta to form a solid and even parcel less than one inch thick (but not too thin), making sure there are no knots or lumps in the muslin that would cause dents in the cheese. Place this on a baking sheet, chopping board or flat dinner plate and cover it with another baking sheet, plate or chopping board, then add five pounds (2kg) of weight on top of that - this can easily be achieved with canning jars filled with water, or with some tins of food. Leave this to press for at least a couple of hours, or overnight, before using in recipes or storing for later.

Some more whey will come out of the curds during the pressing process, so be sure that your baking sheet has a rim around it to contain this, or place it on the draining board of the sink or somewhere else where it can drip. Alternatively, you can just tilt the plates over every so often to drain the whey.

How to store and serve:
Ricotta and paneer can be used right away, or can be put in a container with a lid and stored for a week or two in the fridge, or for several months in the freezer.

To cook paneer, cut it into shapes, heat a frying pan over medium-high heat, add some ghee or lard; once it's very hot, add the paneer, cook on one side until it's browned in places, then flip and cook the other side.

Note: Have I added enough acid?
When the right amount of acid has been added, the whey should be translucent and not at all milky. If your whey appears milky, or if it hasn't distinctly separated into curds and whey at the correct temperature, add more vinegar or lemon juice, gently reheat if needed.

Note: Making ricotta with soured milk, whey, or yoghurt
Another way of making acid-curdled cheeses is to heat up some normal milk, as you would for a vinegar-curdled cheese, Heat it as high as possible first, as the soured milk will make the temperature drop. Once the milk is hot, add soured milk, whey, or yoghurt as you would for vinegar.

The amount to add will vary depending on how sour it is, but you will need a lot more of this than you would for vinegar - around one or two litres (one or two quarts) of sour milk for four litres (one gallon) of fresh milk, if in doubt just mix through a small amount at a time, and if it doesn't curdle, add some more, while keeping the temperature high. This method usually makes more fragile curds than the vinegar method, so is better suited to ricotta than paneer.

Yoghurt cheese
Simple cultured soft cheese

Another good recipe to begin with is to simply get some natural yoghurt made without any thickeners (the ingredients should just be milk and cultures, although yoghurt with added milk solids or added cream will still work for this) or some of your own yoghurt (see page 120). Greek yoghurt will yield more cheese and less whey than thinner yoghurts.

Method

1. Ferment

Firstly, allow your yoghurt to sit at room temperature until the whey has separated from the curds. If you eat a spoon of yoghurt out of it, later in the day, a light green or yellow whey will show where the spoonful was removed. For thinner yoghurts, the yoghurt will stay together in a clump when the jar is tilted, sometimes you will also see a tiny amount of whey when you do this. If your thin yoghurt does not separate after quite some time, you can try either shaking it briefly and then leaving it again, or gently heating it up to 38°C (100°F), which may make the curds and whey more distinct.

2. Strain

Next, place a large freshly-boiled piece of cheesecloth or other thin cloth over a colander and drain the yoghurt over a bowl at around 21°C (70°F) until no more whey drips from it, usually between twelve and twenty four hours. In hot weather it will drain more readily, in cold weather it may slow down a lot, so try to keep it in a warm place.

For best results, tie the cheesecloth up from all four corners and hang it from a wooden spoon over a tall saucepan, making sure it won't be sitting in whey. This will extract more of the whey than using a colander, but it's also a bit harder to begin with, as some of the yoghurt can easily get squeezed out of the cloth when you're tying it. I will often use both methods, starting out the draining in a colander, and then once a good amount of whey has drained, I will tie the

Ingredients
Natural yoghurt without additives

Optional salt, to taste

Equipment
Cheesecloth
Colander

corners up to continue the draining.

3. Salt
Once the cheese is drained, add salt to taste, then hang it back up again for a few hours to allow the salt to drain more of the whey out, or use it right away as a spread. It will get a bit saltier as the liquid drains out, so err on the side of too little salt over too much; you can always add more later.

How to store and serve:
If the curd formed is firm enough (you may need to hang it for a bit longer), you can then roll the cheese into balls and marinate these in some olive oil to help preserve them, this is often done with the addition of some dried herbs or spices added for extra flavour, you can also use yoghurt cheese right away in cheesecakes, dips, and other recipes.

Yoghurt cheese (also known as labneh) has a very sharp and yoghurt-like taste, and is best complemented by other strong flavours, such as dukkah, za'atar, or other nut and spice mixtures. Soft labneh can be drizzled with olive oil, sprinkled with spices and served as a spread with vegetable sticks, roasted vegetables, or flatbread. In sweet dishes it is complemented by honey.

The whey from yoghurt cheese can be used as for any cultured cheese whey, so making this cheese can be a quick way to get some whey ready for making lacto-fermented vegetables.

The whey and the cheese will keep for around two weeks in the fridge, or for several months at fridge or cheese cave conditions if stored in olive oil.

Farmers cheese, bakers cheese, clabber, and quark

Sometimes farmers cheese made from just raw milk and nothing else is too easy to make, other times it just isn't possible. In winter it can be hard to find a temperature warm enough for slowly culturing the milk, whereas in summer in a warm place, the milk will sometimes curdle on its own in 24 hours.

Often these cheeses are made from skimmed milk, which helps prevent off-flavours developing during the long wild fermentation.

Method

1. Ferment
To make this cheese, just set a jar of raw milk at a warm room temperature (preferably around 22°C (71°F) until it turns into curds and whey (around 48 hours). If after that time it still has not separated, gently heat it to 38°C (100°F) to encourage the curds to separate.

2. Strain, salt, and serve
Strain through cheesecloth for a few hours, ideally also at around 22°C (71°F), add salt, to taste, and you have a cheese.

Serve farmers cheese as you would yoghurt cheese: use in cheesecakes and other recipes, or serve as a dip or spread.

For more consistent results, add a small amount of some sort of starter culture, such as viili, kefir or whey, at the rate of around 2 tablespoons starter to 1 litre milk, before culturing and straining as you would for plain raw milk.

A Spotlight on Chèvre
and other slow-cultured cheeses

Chèvre is a lactic curd cheese. The tiniest amount of rennet is added, along with a regular dose of culture, and the cheese is slowly coagulated with the rennet as the culture transforms large amounts of lactose into lactic acid.

There is a massive variety of these cheeses in France, either used fresh, or aged in various ways. Some of them are drained in cheesecloth, as for the basic chèvre recipe, others are delicately ladled into small moulds and then aged.

When this style of cheese is made with cows milk, it's sometimes known as "fromage blanc", and it is quite bland compared to chèvre, but still an excellent cheese to make. Cream cheese is made in a similar way, replacing half the milk with cream.

The beauty of these cheeses is that they can fit into busy lives. If you are away from the house for long hours, there's no need to worry about not being there to cut curds, stir, or any other processes – you can just mix it all up in the morning, leave it for the day, and come back to it at night or the next morning. If you use clean milk, they are very forgiving about being left alone for long hours – sometimes I forget to drain mine, or I don't jar or shape it, and the next morning or night it is still there waiting for me.

I make these cheeses often with fresh goats milk, where I either use them as a fresh spreadable cheese, or age them in various ways. A chèvre moulded by hand can be left to air dry and form nice crumbly cheese for grating. If you want a bloomy white cheese such as Valençay, these cheeses can be ladled into moulds and treated to encourage white moulds, with or without the addition of vegetable ash. Stored in olive oil and herbs, they will keep in cheese cave or fridge conditions for months, yielding a soft spreadable cheese in the depths of winter plus some nicely flavoured oil for salad dressings. Soft chèvre also freezes well in jars.

A key word to remember about these cheeses is *delicate*. They are delicate cheeses, to be treated gently. Another important thing to remember is to use very clean fresh milk – these are the first cheeses to let you know if you have a coliform contamination in your milk. These are ideally cheeses for the homesteader or peasant – do the milking and morning chores, add the culture and rennet, and then leave it alone while getting on with life, returning to the cheese anywhere between 12 and 48 hours later.

Easy Chèvre, Fromage Blanc, or Cream Cheese

Here is my chèvre recipe that I make a lot. Tasting it, you would never know that it's been made just by shaking some ingredients in a jar and ignoring it on a kitchen bench. While this recipe is at its best made with goats milk, you can make it with any kind of milk, it just won't have as much flavour of its own and is perfect with some fresh herbs added; you can also use half cream and half milk, for cream cheese.

It's a lot easier to make a larger batch of chèvre than it is a smaller one, but smaller ones naturally make a smaller amount of cheese that is easier to eat before it starts to go bad. Another advantage of a small batch is that it can be made when you only have a small amount of milk to spare. If you have a lot of milk, feel free to make a larger batch. I've kept the ingredients for this recipe to two litres, which is somewhere in the middle of these sizes. You can halve this recipe if you don't have much milk or many people to feed; you just need to be especially careful about the amount of rennet, as it's very easy to put too much rennet into a small batch of chèvre.

For best results with chèvre, try to keep the temperature at around 22°C (71°F). Significantly higher temperatures will result in faster coagulation with less acidity and flavour. Temperatures as low as 16°C (61°F) will still work well.

Ingredients
2 litres (2 quarts) milk (use goat milk for chèvre)

2 tablespoons (30ml) milk kefir, viili, or fresh whey

1 tiny, tiny amount of rennet (see the method for details)

1 teaspoon unrefined salt without additives, or more to taste

Equipment
Jar or pot for culturing the cheese
Cheesecloth
Colander
Wooden spoon for hanging

Method

1. Culture and rennet the milk

Firstly get the milk at a good temperature for culturing. If you're using milk fresh from the udder, allow it to cool down a bit before you begin. If you're using cold milk, heat it up gently on the stove until it reaches a lukewarm temperature, around 72°F (22°C), then add the culture and rennet.

The rennet used for spreadable chèvre is the smallest amount possible. Too much rennet will result in a rubbery curd. If you're using rennet tablets, scrape the tiniest tiny speck off a tablet and mix it into some water until it dissolves. If your milk is low in solids or if you think you may have used too much, throw away half this liquid or more. For liquid rennet, mix 1 drop (0.5ml) into some water, and then throw out half of this. If your liquid rennet is double strength, use even less. For powder, measure out 1/64 teaspoon, dilute it, and then only use half of this. It's better to have too little rennet in this recipe than too much.

A little more rennet can be used for ladled curd and crottin-style chèvres, especially if you are making them with thick winter milk, but for soft, spreadable chèvre, use the tiniest amount possible.

When the milk is at the right temperature, add the diluted rennet and the culture and gently but thoroughly mix it into the milk. Leave it to set at room temperature for twelve to forty eight hours, until the curd has separated from the whey (ideally the curd will be covered by around 1cm (½") of whey). You can leave it for a bit longer if you like, or less time if it has set quickly. I think the best flavour develops between 24 and 36 hours.

If the room temperature has dropped below 16°C (61°F) overnight during the slow coagulation time, you may need to leave your chèvre culturing for longer, as the culturing and coagulating halts when the temperature gets too low and starts up again in warmer temperatures.

2. Drain, salt, and serve

When the curd is ready, gently pour the curds and whey into a colander lined with cheesecloth, or ladle into forms. You can then tie the four corners of the cheesecloth onto a wooden spoon and leave it to drain.

Draining will take around eight hours at 22°C (72°F), it will be faster in warmer temperatures, slower in cooler weather. For the best flavour, try to keep the temperature as close to 22°C (72°F) as possible. Once the cheese has drained, add some salt to taste, and either use right away as a spread, or drain for another couple of hours, to make a firmer cheese that stays fresh for longer.

During the draining phase it can be a good idea to taste your cheese every so often – if it tastes like it has cultured enough but hasn't drained for long enough to store well, just add the salt now and continue the draining, as the salt will help to drain the curd while slowing the culturing.

Chèvre will keep for a week or two in the fridge, or in a cool larder for a few days, or can also be frozen for several months.

The many ways of aging chèvre

Making chèvre is so simple and easy to fit into a busy life, especially if you love soft cheeses. To turn this delicious and simple cheese into an aged cheese, there are several ways of taking some more simple steps to get the cheese ready for aging. For many of these methods it is even possible to just follow the standard chèvre directions, and then divide up the drained curds and use some for fresh eating and some for aging.

Aged chèvres can be eaten any time, depending on what your goals are. If you want some soft cheese without much aging, you can eat them quickly. If you are after mould development, you'll need to wait at least a couple of weeks. If you want a nice dry grating cheese, waiting a month or longer will help. Once the rind has developed correctly, the aged chèvre will keep for much longer than this, it will just continue drying out and changing texture, with the air-dried crottins storing exceptionally well as dry grating cheeses, and bloomy rinds storing nicely at cold temperatures when wrapped in parchment baking paper or leaves.

Crottin

To make a Crottin style of aged chèvre, just follow the chèvre directions above, draining in cheesecloth, but try not to add any salt to the curds. Once your curds have been drained in the cheesecloth, either hand mould them into small cylinders roughly two inches wide by an inch and a half in height, or gently pack into small round cheese forms for 24 hours, flipping halfway through.

If you want to hand mould this cheese but your chèvre is having trouble draining, mix a small amount of salt into the curds and allow to drain for a further two to six hours, making sure your draining temperature is as close to 22°C (72°F) as possible, as low temperatures will inhibit draining, then reduce the amount of salt used when salting the surface. Another trick for hand moulding is to use a piece of cheesecloth to shape your cheeses by gathering the cheesecloth up around each cheese and twisting it from above to lightly press the cheese together.

Lightly salt the surface of the cheese. For bloomy rinds, use around 2.5g (¾ of a teaspoon) unrefined salt for every 100g (3.5oz) crottin, use slightly more salt for an air-dried rind. Dry in a cool airy place for a day, or until the surface has firmed up a little, flipping once or twice per day, before aging at 10-12°C (50°F-54°F) with high humidity for two to four weeks, to encourage moulds to develop.

Once enough mould has developed for your liking, either eat them right away, or wrap in beeswax wrap or parchment baking paper and continue aging at low temperatures.

Air-dried chèvre

Follow the crottin directions, above, but age your cheese at around 10-18°C (50°F-64°F) with lower-than-ideal cheese cave humidity, to dry the rind without developing much mould. A cheese made this way and aged for a month or more can be finely grated and used as a substitute for Parmesan and other hard grating cheeses. It stores very well. Crottin made in natural conditions in dry summer months often turns out in this way.

Aged chèvre with a herbed, spiced, or ashed rind

Follow the directions for making a regular batch of chèvre, salting and further draining the curds to form an easily handmoulded cheese. Form the cheese into rounds with your hands or using cheesecloth, as you would for crottin. Roll your cheeses in your choice of dried crumbled nettle or other dried herbs, smoked paprika, a mix of spices, or vegetable ash. Dry in a cool airy place, flipping once or twice per day, before aging at 10-12°C (50°F-54°F) for a couple of days or for longer.

Ladled curd aged chèvre

Several French goat cheeses are made in this manner, where the chèvre is slowly cultured in the jar or vat, as for the standard soft chèvre recipe above, but instead of draining in cheesecloth, the curd is gently ladled into small cheese forms and left alone to drain in the form for around 24 hours, with no flipping, ideally at a temperature of between 20°C and 22°C (68°F to 72°F).

The cheese is then gently unmoulded, salted, and then placed first in a cool airy place, flipping once or twice per day, for a day or two, before aging at 10-12°C (50°F-54°F) with high humidity for two to four weeks, to encourage moulds to develop.

Cheeses made in this way will age differently, depending on the shape and size of the form. Smaller forms will hold the curds made from just half a litre (2 cups) of milk, most forms will hold the curds from one litre or quart, and some are slightly larger, holding curds from a two litre batch. Some forms, such as the pyramid shape, will need to be topped up with more curds one to three times in the first hour after filling, other forms, such as tall cylinders, can simply be filled with curds and left to drain, as they will shrink down into the preferred smaller shape on their own.

Some ladled curd chèvres will be sprinkled with vegetable charcoal before aging, to encourage different surface bacteria, others are surface salted and then either left as they are in high humidity, or gently washed for a couple of days with salted whey to keep the surface moist and encourage moulds to colonise the surface.

Age as you would for any aged cheese, moving to a dry space once or twice a day for the first week, and for all except pyramid forms, flipping the cheese over as you do this. To encourage white moulds, see the section on bloomy white rind cheeses on page 104.

Leaf-wrapped chèvre

Choose non-toxic leaves such as chestnut, maple, walnut, grape, or nettle. For nettle, you'll need to blanch the leaves briefly in boiling water or freeze them to remove the sting, other leaves can be used either raw, blanched, or soaked in brandy or whiskey for a week. Follow the directions for making crottin, making rounds or small logs that can easily be rolled up in your leaves of choice. Salt the outside of your cheeses and allow the rind to air-dry for a couple of days before wrapping each cheese in a leaf, securing the edges with raffia or other string.

Leaves can also be used to wrap a bloomy rind cheese after the white moulds have started to grow.

Chèvre in oil

Another way to preserve chèvre or yoghurt cheese is to preserve it in oil. Olive oil is the traditional choice and adds extra flavour but it can congeal at cold temperatures. Cold-pressed sunflower oil can be used instead. Dried herbs and spices can be added to the oil to infuse the cheese with different flavours, just be careful to avoid fresh herbs and garlic as these can cause botulism.

To preserve chèvre in oil, follow the chèvre recipe above, salting and draining for a further two hours or more, to remove more of the whey. Mould your chèvre into small rounds, roughly an inch and a half to two inches in size, and if they are quite firm you can put them in oil now. If your cheeses are still very delicate, you can create a small rind on them by air drying them as-is for a day or two, or rolling in dried herbs and then air drying them.

To put your chèvre in oil, start with a layer of oil in a jar, and an optional small sprinkling of dried herbs, put your cheeses into the oil, making sure they are not touching, then fill with more oil and optional herbs, adding more cheeses until you've run out of cheese. Top with a layer of oil, to make sure the cheeses are completely covered, then put the lid on. Chèvre in oil will keep in a cool place for several months.

Once you've eaten the chèvre, the oil can be used for salad dressings and other purposes.

Fast Mozzarella: Simple everyday pizza cheese

There are two methods for making mozzarella. The first is to culture it slowly to develop the right amount of acidity to allow it to stretch. The second method is to add the acid as vinegar or lemon juice, at the right stage of the recipe. The first method will have more flavour, but is a sometimes unreliable process, the second makes a great cheese for pizza in around forty five minutes.

Making mozzarella the fast way means that if your family likes pizza and other melty cheese dishes, you can easily provide for this at home. It's possible to make fast mozzarella while the oven heats up and the dough rises, or to use milk that is older than ideal for cultured cheesemaking.

Vinegar added to hot milk results in ricotta, so be sure to add the vinegar to your milk for mozzarella when cold or at room temperature.

This recipe makes enough mozzarella for one or two large pizzas. Feel free to double or triple the recipe to make more. Mozzarella freezes well.

Method

1. Add vinegar to milk, then warm it
Gently stir the vinegar into the milk before the heating begins. Heat the milk gently on the stove, while stirring often to a lukewarm temperature of around 32°C (90°F).

2. Add rennet
Dissolve the rennet in around 1/4 cup of water, stir it constantly and

Ingredients
2 litres (2 quarts) milk

60ml (1/4 cup) cider vinegar

1/8 rennet tablet, 1/64 teaspoon powdered rennet, or 1/8 teaspoon liquid rennet

2 tablespoons unrefined salt without additives

Equipment
Pot with at least 2 litre (2 quart) capacity
Thermometer (optional)
Knife for cutting curds
Colander
Bowl for catching whey
Slotted spoon
A second spoon, either metal or wooden

then quickly and thoroughly mix it through all the milk for a minute or two in an up and down motion. Stir for two minutes, then leave the pot alone for 5 minutes.

3. Cut curds
Check to see if a curd has formed (this usually takes around 5 to 10 minutes). When the curd forms and breaks cleanly, cut it into one inch cubes.

4. Heat and stir
Put the pot back on the heat and heat it to around 43°C (110°F) while stirring the curds. Remove it from the heat and continue to stir the curds for two to five minutes.

5. Drain
Drain the curds into a colander, catching the whey with a bowl underneath and then putting it back in the pot.

6. Heat whey
Add 2 tablespoons salt to the whey and heat it until it reaches a temperature of at least 175°F (80°C) but is not boiling.

7. Stretch
Take handfuls of the drained curd, place on the slotted spoon, and lower into the hot whey for a few seconds, then use the slotted spoon with a second spoon to stretch and knead the curd several times, to develop strings, lowering it back into the whey in between kneads and stretches, before forming into a ball shape.

The amount of stretching to give it is completely up to you - sometimes I barely stretch at all (see the note below for more on this), other times I stretch until my hands are quite far apart with a long string of mozzarella stretching between them, which is closer in mind to what the mozzarella purists want, but a bit more time consuming to achieve.

The two important things about stretching are firstly, that it really does not matter that much, your cheese will be tasty and edible whether it stretches or not, and secondly not to break it. Allow it to soften enough before you start stretching, and it starts looking like it's about to break and you want to keep stretching, put it back in the whey before trying again.

If it isn't stretchy enough for you and keeps wanting to break, try to put it in the hot whey for a bit longer before stretching again, or increasing the whey temperature. At some times of the seasonal milk cycle, mozzarella just doesn't stretch as well; it will still taste great though.

Continue the heating and stretching for the rest of the curds, draining them as you go.

How to store and serve:
Fast mozzarella can be used right away, or will keep in the fridge for around a week. It can also be frozen for several months. For best results if you'll be storing your mozzarella, drain the stretched curds for several hours in a bundle of cheesecloth hanging from a wooden spoon, as you would for chèvre, to allow any excess moisture to drain before storing.

For faster mozzarella:
Instead of doing all the stretching, you can still make an acceptable pizza mozzarella that isn't as stretchy by instead heating the salty whey until fairly hot, and immersing the whole curd mass at once in it. Allow to sit for a couple of minutes, to soften and absorb salt, and you can optionally knead it a bit if it has softened enough, or simply remove and drain it.

Slow Cultured Mozzarella

Making a slow cultured mozzarella starts in a similar way to many hard cheeses – culture, rennet, cutting, stirring. The cheese is then allowed to further acidify until it gets to just the right level of acidity for stretching. It's not possible to know the exact pH without expensive pH test strips or an electric gadget, but fortunately there are ways to test your cheese to see if it is ready and make a great mozzarella without knowing the pH.

A pH of between 5.2 and 4.6 allows your mozzarella to stretch to perfection, but with further acidification beyond 4.6, the curds will not stretch (but they will still melt). The key to making great cultured mozzarella is to be able to test the curd every so often to see if it's ready to stretch.

To test for stretching, take a 1 inch piece of curd, immerse it in water at 80°C (175°F) or above, then knead it in your hands and begin to stretch, putting it back in the hot water before stretching again – if there is a lot of stretch then it's ready, if you're not sure, put it back in the hot water and knead a couple more times.

Patience also helps to make a good cultured mozzarella – sometimes it will reliably stretch after 90 minutes, other times it will take much longer. To make for more predictable stretching, be sure to keep the temperature as close to 38°C (100°F) as possible. If you have to go to bed or go out and your mozzarella still isn't ready, put it in a cold place such as a fridge or larder and this will halt the acid development – to start it up again just move your cheese back to 38°C (100°F) and keep going.

Ripening time: 1 hour
Rennetting time: 1 hour
Stirring time: 1 hour
Acidifying time: 90 minutes or longer

Ingredients
4 litres (1 gallon) milk

60ml (1/4 cup) yoghurt or milk kefir

1/4 rennet tablet, 1/32 teaspoon powdered rennet, or 1/4 teaspoon liquid rennet

1 tablespoon unrefined salt without additives

Equipment
Pot at least 4 litres (1 gallon) in size
Spoon
Thermometer (optional)
Knife for cutting curds
Colander
Cheesecloth
Pot or bowl, for catching whey

Method

1. Culture
Gently heat your milk to a lukewarm temperature of around 32°C (90°F). Thoroughly mix through the yoghurt and allow it to ripen for

60 minutes.

2. Add rennet

Dissolve the rennet in ¼ cup of water, stir it constantly and then pour it over the cultured milk. Quickly and thoroughly mix it through all the milk for a minute or two with an up and down motion, then leave it to sit for another 60 minutes, until there is a clean break in the curd.

3. Cut curds, heat, and stir

Once the curd has set, cut it into 1cm (1/2") cubes. Leave to rest for 10 minutes before slowly increasing the temperature to 38°C (100°F), stirring every so often for 60 minutes.

4. Drain whey, keep curds warm

Drain the whey from the curds, reserving 1 litre (1 quart) for later in the recipe. Put the curds back in the pot and keep in a warm place, such as a sink full of warm water, or the non-hotplate edge of a wood stove, ideally keeping the temperature at around 38°C (100°F) during this time (lower temperatures will mean slower ripening).

Allow your cheese to ripen and develop acidity, removing built-up whey every so often, until it passes the stretch test (this may happen in 90 minutes, or it may take hours). To test for stretching, take a 1 inch piece of curd, immerse it in water at around 80°C (175°F) or above, then knead it in your hands and begin to stretch, putting it back in the hot water before stretching again – if there is a lot of stretch then it's ready, if you're not sure, put it back in the hot water and knead a couple more times, increasing the temperature if needed, or leaving it in the water for longer.

Sometimes in the seasonal milking cycle, mozzarella will not stretch as well – if you have been ripening your mozzarella at the right temperature for a long time, and it is kneading but not properly stretching, this may be the case, feel free to just heat the whey now, knead and stretch as far as it will go without breaking and call it a day. It will still taste great even if it doesn't stretch properly!

5. Stretch

Once your cheese is ready to stretch, heat the reserved 1 litre (1 quart) of whey to 77°C-82°C (170 to 180°F) and add 1 tablespoon salt. Take handfuls of the drained curd, place on the slotted spoon, and lower into the hot whey for a few seconds, then use the slotted spoon with a second spoon to stretch and knead the curd several times, to develop strings, before forming into a ball shape. If it isn't stretchy at this point, try to put it in the hot whey for a bit longer before trying again.

Continue this for the rest of the curds, draining them as you go.

How to store and serve

Mozzarella can be used right away, frozen, stored as-is in the fridge for a week, or make a brine as you would for feta (page 90), and store your mozzarella in that in a fridge or cheese cave for up to three weeks. If storing in the fridge or freezer, I'd recommend draining the stretched curds in cheesecloth tied from a wooden spoon for at least a couple of hours, to allow excess moisture to drain.

Quick method for experienced cheesemakers:

Culture 32°C (90°F) 60 minutes.
Rennet 60 minutes.
Cut 1cm (½") curds).
Stir 38°C (100°F) 60 minutes.
Drain. Reserve 1 litre whey.
Ripen curds at 38°C (100°F) until they stretch, at least 90 minutes.
Heat 1 litre whey with 1 tablespoon salt to 77-82°C (170-180°F). Stretch curds in hot whey.

Focusing of feta and other brined cheeses

Brined cheeses come from countries near the Mediterranean Sea, where temperatures can get quite hot, but there is plentiful salt to help with food preservation.

If you struggle with finding the right conditions to age other cheeses, brined cheeses may become a staple cheese for you. They can be aged in warm conditions, or can be slowly aged at fridge temperatures, and because they are aged in jars, there is no need to worry about having any particular humidity in the room.

The brine used to preserve these cheeses can either be a plain salt and water brine, or a whey brine. I prefer the whey brine, as it has extra minerals that prevent the feta from disintegrating, and it adds extra flavour. Cheesemakers who use the plain salt and water brine will sometimes use calcium chloride to add these extra minerals to the brine instead, but as I can easily produce whey on my homestead but not calcium chloride, I prefer to use whey.

The brine in the feta recipe is a 4% brine, which means a ratio of 40 grams unrefined salt to 1 litre of whey. This brine is ideal for keeping feta as a storable staple cheese in hotter than ideal temperatures, or in good cheese cave temperatures for a year or more. If you prefer a less-salty feta and will be storing it in a fridge or eating it quickly, feel free to reduce the amount of salt in the brine by one tablespoon.

Greek Feta is probably the most famous of the brined cheeses: crumbly, salty, and full of flavour, feta can be brined from anywhere from a few days to a year or more. Some cheesemakers prefer to produce a more tender curd and to allow it to press under its own weight, but I prefer to use some pressure from a jar of water to be extra sure that I get strong feta that will not fall apart in the brine.

Bulgarian Feta is less well known, with a smoother, creamier texture, and is well worth making. If you want to make this style of feta, simply follow the feta recipe on the following page, cutting the curds into larger two to three inch slabs, and then instead of stirring, rest the curds for ten minutes before gently ladling them into a cheesecloth-lined colander to pre-drain for a few hours, then transferring the bundle to a cheese mould with follower and pressing with around 1kg (2 pounds) of weight for three hours or so.

Halloumi is a completely different cheese from feta, but it is also stored in brine to add flavour and preserve the cheese. Halloumi can be cut into cubes and threaded onto a stick with a mixture of fast-cooking vegetables to be cooked on the barbecue or grill for kebabs, or it can be sliced, then fried or grilled, and added to all kinds of salads, sandwiches, and platters, or served as a tasty snack on its own.

All of these cheeses are traditionally made from goat or sheep milk rather than cows milk. They can be made from cows milk at home, but they will end up milder in flavour. The best flavour comes from the milk of sheep or goats that are eating from rough land with plenty of woody plants and weeds.

Because these cheeses are aged in brine, they don't need to be any particular size or shape. I've included recipes using just two litres (half a gallon) of milk, but you can double or triple all the ingredients to make a larger batch.

Feta

Feta is a semi-hard cheese that's traditionally aged in a salty whey brine. Below 15°C (60°F) is ideal for aging feta, but I find that even in warmer-than-ideal temperatures I can store feta for many months.

Feta develops more flavour as it ages in the brine, so the pressing time can be quite flexible. If you will be aging your feta in the fridge rather than a cheese cave, don't add the salt to the curds and make sure to press overnight (or longer), as less flavour will develop during aging at these low temperatures. If you will be aging your feta at higher temperatures, adding salt to the curds will help it to store, and pressing doesn't need to go for as long. If you are working with cows milk, ideally don't add salt to the curds, and allow it to press overnight or longer, as cows milk feta will not develop as much flavour as feta made from goat or sheep milk.

Method

1. Culture
Gently heat your milk to a lukewarm temperature of around 32°C (90°F), thoroughly mix through the kefir, then leave it to sit for an hour to ripen.

2. Add rennet
Dissolve the rennet in ¼ cup of water, stir it constantly and then pour it over the cultured milk. Quickly and thoroughly mix it through all the milk for a minute or two with an up and down motion, then leave it to sit for another hour, until there is a clean break in the curd.

3. Cut curds and stir
Once the curd has set, cut it into 3/4" (2cm) cubes. Stir the curds every few minutes for the next 30 to 60 minutes, until they are firmer and slightly springy. Try to keep the temperature as close to 32°C (90°F) as you can while you do this - a lower temperature will result in a slower process.

Ripening time: 1 hour
Rennetting time: 1 hour
Stirring time: 30-60 minutes
First pressing: 30 minutes
Second pressing: 10 minutes or overnight

Ingredients

2 litres (half a gallon) non-homogenised milk

2 tablespoons (30ml) viili, milk kefir, or fresh whey

Rennet: 1/8 tablet, 1/64 teaspoon powdered, or 1/8 teaspoon liquid

Additive-free salt

Equipment
Pot at least 2 litres (half gallon) in size
Spoon
Thermometer (optional)
Knife for cutting curds
Pot or bowl, for catching whey
Colander
Cheesecloth
Glass jar, with glass or plastic lid, at least 500ml or 1 pint in size
***Optional cheese mould with follower and a jar for weight

4. Drain

Stop stirring and allow the curds to settle to the bottom of the pot, then pour the whey into a different pot or bowl; make sure to keep 350ml (1½ cups) of this for the aging brine.

Drain the rest of the curds through a colander lined with cheesecloth, then mix through an optional tablespoon of unrefined salt. Leave the curds to drain for around five minutes, stirring a couple of times to stop the curds sticking together too much.

5. Press

Put cheesecloth in your cheese mould and put the salted curds in here; gently cover the cheese with the cloth, then the follower, and then 1½kg (3 pounds) of weight (a jar filled with water works well), for around 30 minutes. Unwrap the cheese, flip it over, rewrap (see page 55 for details), and press it for at least 10 more minutes, preferably overnight.

6. Make brine

While you're waiting for the cheese to press, you can make the brine by dissolving 1½ tablespoons of unrefined salt without additives into 350ml (1½ cups) of warm whey. Set this aside until later.

Once the pressing has finished, taste a little of the feta and see if you think it has enough flavour. If it is lacking in flavour, feel free to put it back in the press and allow it to keep pressing for another 6 hours.

7. Cut and age

Cut the cheese into pieces, either slabs or large cubes, whichever will fit in your brining container (don't cut them into little cubes like feta in jars in the shops, or you're likely to lose a lot of your cheese).

Put the feta pieces in the brine and ideally store it below 10°C (50°F). It will be best if you can wait at least a week before eating it, longer is even better. You can get away with storing it at a warmer temperature if you eat it earlier and don't store it for long.

If your cheese floats in the jar and is exposed to air, use a sterilised glass or stone weight in the jar to weigh it down, or sprinkle with a layer of salt.

Note: ***If you don't have a cheese mould, you can just hang the unsalted feta up in a cheesecloth, with the corners tied on a wooden spoon, and drain it for 24 hours. Try to first shape it into a log or round before draining, to help keep it in one piece. Made this way, the feta will not be as firm as the pressed version, and may need to be handled carefully, but it still tastes great and ages in brine well. If you have trouble with it crumbling in the brine, in your next batch, after draining, carefully cut it into 2" cubes, then sprinkle with a little salt and allow them to air dry for 24 hours in a dry place, flipping over partway through, to allow the edges to form a rind, then add to the brine.

Quick-glance method for experienced cheesemakers:

Culture at 32°C for 60 minutes.
Rennet 60 minutes.
Cut 2cm (3/4") curds, stir 30-60 minutes at 32°C.
Drain curds into cheesecloth, reserving 350ml (1 ½ cups) for the brine.
Optionally mix 1 tablespoon salt into curds.
Put curds into mould.
Press with jar 30 minutes.
Flip and press 10 minutes to 16 hours.

Halloumi: Salty grilling cheese

Rennetting time: 40-60 minutes
Stirring time: 20 minutes
First pressing: 30 minutes
Second pressing: 30 minutes
Heating time: 30-40 minutes

Halloumi is another cheese that can be aged in brine. Fresh or aged, it can be fried or put on a BBQ to form a tasty sandwich filling or snack with an irresistible, slightly squeaky, chewy, almost meaty texture.

The reason halloumi does not melt when heated is because it is quite low in acid from the fast cheesemaking process that uses minimal (or no) added culture, along with the process of heating the pressed cheese in whey that halts any further acid development and gives halloumi its lovely chewy texture.

Method

1. Add rennet
Gently heat your milk to a lukewarm temperature of around 90°F (32°C). Dilute the rennet in ¼ cup of water, stir it constantly, then add this to the milk, along with the optional kefir, and thoroughly mix it through for a minute or two in an up and down motion. Leave to set for around 40 minutes to an hour, until the curd cleanly breaks.

2. Cut curds
Cut the curd into one inch (2.5cm) cubes.

3. Heat and stir
Increase the temperature to around 38°C (100°F) while stirring often to make sure the curds don't stick to the pot. Keep the cheese at this temperature for another 20 minutes, while stirring every so often, until they are firm and slightly springy.

4. Drain and press:
Allow the curds to settle for 5 minutes, before pouring off the whey into another pot or bowl to use later in this recipe.

Put the curds into a cheesecloth, inside a cheese mould, top with the

Ingredients
2 litres (half a gallon) milk

Optional 1 tablespoon milk kefir, viili, yoghurt, or fresh whey

1/8 tablet rennet, 1/64 teaspoon powdered rennet, or 1/8 teaspoon liquid rennet

Equipment
Pot with at least 2 litre (half gallon) capacity

Spoon

Knife for cutting curds

Cheesecloth

Bowl or pot for catching whey

Optional cheese mould, follower, and weight

follower, and then with some weight to help it press, such as a quart or litre jar filled with water. Leave it to press for around an hour, flipping it over halfway through by removing the cheesecloth, rewrapping, and pressing with the other side of the cheese down (see page 55 for details). Alternatively, if you don't have a cheese mould, press as you would for paneer, page 73.

5. Heat whey and scald cheese

While the cheese is pressing, heat the whey up until almost-boiling (around 90°C/195°F) and allow ricotta curds to form on top. Remove the ricotta. then add the pressed halloumi and leave it in the hot whey, making sure it doesn't boil, until the cheese rises to the surface. This will take around 30-40 minutes. It may still feel soft when it is in the whey, but it will firm up once it's cooled - if you're unsure you can check for firmness by slicing off a bit of curd and allowing it to cool to room temperature - when it's ready it will be firm, like cooked chicken breast meat.

How to store and serve:

The cheese can now be cooled, and either sprinkled with salt and fried right away (or kept for a few days in the fridge), or stored in a 5% brine. It will store in the brine for longer if kept under 10°C (50°F), but warmer temperatures are fine too, for a shorter time.

To make a 5% brine, use 50 grams of salt to a litre of whey or water, or 5 tablespoons per quart.

Quick-glance method for experienced cheesemakers:

Rennet 40 to 60 minutes.
Cut 2.5cm (1") curds.
Bring to 38°C (100°F).
Hold at 38°C (100°F) 20 minutes.
Press with jar 60 minutes, flipping halfway through.
Heat whey to 90°C (195°F), put cheese in there until it rises.

Tomme: Simple homesteader's hard cheese

Tomme is a hard cheese which can be made without a cheese press, and the simplest hard cheese to make.

The taste of this cheese can not be judged by the simplicity of making it – it has a wonderful depth of flavour, and as it is not as familiar to us as some other hard cheeses are, we don't have much of an expectation of what it should taste like, and can appreciate it more for what it is rather than trying to compare it with other cheeses.

Tomme has some similarities in its taste to Alpine cheeses, with a complex, pleasant and satisfying taste that lends itself well to being sliced thinly and appreciated on its own, or used anywhere you would use a hard cheese.

Method

1. Culture
Gently heat your milk to a lukewarm temperature of around 90°F (32°C), thoroughly mix through the kefir, then leave it to sit for an hour to ripen.

2. Rennet
Dissolve the rennet in half a cup of water, stir it constantly and then pour it over the cultured milk. Quickly and thoroughly mix it through all the milk for a minute or two in an up and down motion, then leave it to sit for another hour, until there is a clean break in the curd.

3. Cut curds
Cut the curd into small cubes, around 1/5 of an inch (half a centimetre) in size. Allow the curds to rest for five minutes.

Ripening time: 1 hour
Rennetting time: 1 hour
Stirring time: 35-60 minutes
First pressing: 30 minutes
Second pressing: 12-24 hours

Ingredients
5 or 6 litres (6 quarts) non-homogenised milk

80ml (1/3 cup) milk kefir, viili, or fresh whey

1/2 tablet rennet, 1/16 teaspoon powdered rennet, or 1/2 teaspoon liquid rennet

Additive-free salt

Equipment
Pot with at least 6 litre (6 quart) capacity

Spoon

Knife for cutting curds

Cheesecloth

800g (5" wide) cheese mould, follower, and weight

4. Heat and stir

Slowly heat the curds to 38°C (100°F) over the course of half an hour, stirring often to make sure the curds don't clump together or stick to the bottom of the pot.

Maintain the temperature of 38°C (100°F), while stirring every so often. After around 5 minutes, begin testing the feel of the curds - they should feel slightly springy when squeezed. Continue to stir every few minutes while maintaining the temperature until the curds have reached the right texture. It may take up to half an hour.

5. Drain whey

Once the curds have reached the right texture, allow them to settle to the bottom of the pot, and then pour off as much whey from the top as you can.

6. First press

Line the cheese mould with cheesecloth and put the curds into this. Fold the cheesecloth over the top, cover with the follower, then cover with a one litre (1 quart) jar filled with water.

Allow to press for half an hour, then remove the cheese from the cloth, flip it over, rewrap (see page 55 for details), and press again. If you can add more weight to this next pressing it will be better for it, if not, it will not matter so much.

7. Second press

Allow the cheese to press this second time for 12 to 24 hours.

8. Salt

Carefully remove the cheese from the cloth, rub 1½ tablespoons of salt all over it, and allow it to dry in a cool, airy place for 24 to 48 hours, to begin developing a rind.

9. Age

Once the rind has formed, move the cheese to wherever you're aging it.

Age for at least three weeks, rubbing the rind with some salt or a clean dry cloth around once a week. It will develop more flavour the longer it ages, ideally around two to three months. It will become more strongly flavoured, dry, and Parmesan-like at 4 months and beyond.

Quick-glance method for experienced cheesemakers:

Culture at 32°C (90°F) for 60 minutes
Rennet 60 minutes
Cut 5mm (1/5") curds
Stir while heating to 38°C (100°F).
Hold at 38°C (100°F) until curds hold together and feel slightly springy
Drain, press with a 1 litre (1 quart) jar.
Salt with 1 ½ tablespoons salt

The washed curd technique: creating mild and milky cheeses

Earlier in the book I discussed the washed curd technique. Washing the curds removes lactose from the whey, leaving less food for the cultures to feed on and turn into the acid that leaches calcium out of the curd. The end result of this is a mild, milky taste, and a pliable texture that is perfect for sandwiches, salads, and on its own.

Gouda is a cheese that always uses this technique as an essential part of the cheesemaking process, washing the curds with hot water to heat them while removing lactose at the same time.

Gouda was originally made in wooden cheese vats, where the only way to heat the curds was by adding in warm water. This method is a very gentle way to heat the curds, and can be a good one to try if you have trouble regulating the temperature of a cheese pot heated on the stove or water bath.

Recipes for Havarti vary, with some following the same hot water technique as for Gouda, and others washing with water at around 30°C (86°F) shortly after the curds are cut, with all heating of the curds happening from a water bath or stovetop.

These two washed curd cheeses are just great everyday tasty cheeses for sandwiches, salads, snacks, and anywhere that you'd like a mild and milky cheese. Simple to make, fast to age, these are cheeses that I make often as one of the staple cheeses on my homestead. They can be eaten young, as lovely mild cheeses, or aged for longer, where they develop more flavour, dry out, and can be used in many recipes and for grating and slicing.

Washed curd cheeses are perfect vehicles for experimenting with different spices and flavourings. Caraway Gouda and caraway Havarti, pictured opposite, are probably the most well known spiced cheeses, and definitely worth trying if you love the taste of caraway. Cumin seeds, mustard seeds, black peppercorns, and fenugreek are also found sometimes in Gouda.

I've included instructions for making a caraway Havarti variation in the following recipe. To use any other spice in its place, first consider how strong the spice is: caraway is quite distinct and its flavour transfers strongly into the cheese, so only a tiny amount is used, and most spices are used in similar amounts to this.

Beyond Havarti and Gouda there are cheeses that use different washed curd methods. Some, such as Colby and Monterey Jack are washed with cool water after the curds have shrunken during a typical hard cheese heating and stirring process. The curds for these cheeses are then milled and salted, as for Cheddar, and require a cheese press, whereas Havarti and Gouda work well being pressed with a simple jar of water or other light weight.

Washed curd technique can be added into any other hard cheese recipe to achieve certain results. If you are finding that your cheeses are more crumbly and sharper in flavour than you would like, experiment with replacing some of the whey with water to make a milder, more pliable cheese, or if you are a fan of mild milky cheeses, feel free to follow the recipe on the following page to make Gouda and Havarti staple cheeses in your kitchen too!

Havarti and Gouda

Ripening time: 30 to 45 minutes
Rennetting time: 30 to 45 minutes
Stirring time: 20 to 40 minutes
First pressing: 20 minutes
Second pressing: 3 to 8 hours

These cheeses use the washed curd method, which gives the cheese a mild milky taste.

These cheeses don't need much weight, and it's easy to get away with pressing them using jars of water rather than needing a cheese press. Gouda is usually covered in wax before aging, and Havarti is sometimes waxed as well, both these cheeses can easily be made with a natural rind, and that is how I prefer to make them.

Be very careful about the source of water used in this recipe, to make sure you're not adding in any chemicals or bad bacteria. I use creek water or rain water that has been boiled and then cooled.

Ingredients

4 or 5 litres (1 gallon) non-homogenised milk

60ml (1/4 cup) milk kefir, viili or fresh whey

1/4 tablet rennet, 1/32 teaspoon powdered rennet, or 1/4 teaspoon liquid rennet

Hot water, for washing the curds

1 tablespoon additive-free salt

Equipment

Pot or container with at least 5 litre (5 quart) capacity
Spoon
Knife for cutting curds
Cheesecloth
Bowl or pot for catching whey
500g to 800g (5" wide) cheese mould, follower, and weight

Method

1. Culture
Gently heat the milk to 30°C (86°F). Mix the kefir into the milk and leave to ripen for 30 to 45 minutes. Heat the water that you'll use for washing the curds.

2. Rennet
Dissolve the rennet in a quarter cup of water, stir it constantly and then pour it over the cultured milk. Quickly and thoroughly mix it through all the milk for a minute or two in an up and down motion, then leave it to sit for another 30 to 45 minutes, until there is a clean break in the curd.

3. Cut curds and stir
Cut the curds into 1.5cm (½") cubes. Allow the curds to rest for ten minutes, then stir them for five minutes.

4. Wash curds
Remove 1 litre (1 quart) whey. I find it is easiest to do this by first allowing the curds to settle to the bottom of the pot for a minute, then

using a soup ladle with a slotted spoon over the top of it to ladle out whey while stopping curds getting in.

(If you have trouble removing that much whey at once, you can do it over two different stages - the first stage removing 500ml or half a quart of whey, and replacing with the same amount of warm water, and the second stage removing another 500ml or half quart and replacing with warm water.)

Slowly, very slowly, over the course of ten minutes, add 1 litre (1 quart) of water at around 70°C (158°F) back into the cheese pot in small amounts, stirring well in between each addition and avoiding tipping it directly on the curds. Once all the hot water is added, the whey temperature will have increased to around 38°C (100°F).

Check to see if the curds are ready by squeezing a handful of them; they should be slightly springy, and will want to stick together. Keep gently stirring until they feel ready.

5. Press
Once the curds are ready, allow them to settle to the bottom of the whey for five minutes before pouring the whey off and putting the curds into the cheesecloth inside the cheese mould.

Carefully wrap the curds in the cheesecloth, put the follower on top of the cheese mould, then cover with around 1kg (2lb) weight. Press for 20 minutes, then unwrap the cheese, flip, and rewrap, and then press with around 1.5kg (3.5lb) of weight for 3 to 8 hours.

6. Salt
Rub 1 tablespoon unrefined salt over the surface of the cheese, and leave it to dry in a cool, airy place for 24 to 48 hours, to begin developing a rind.

7. Age
Once the rind has formed, move the cheese to your usual cheese aging space. You can begin eating this cheese after three weeks, but it will develop more flavour as it ages for longer.

As the cheese ages, check on it once a week and flip it, rubbing the rind with a clean dry cloth or some salt if there are any unwanted moulds on it.

Notes and variations:

Larger batch:
This recipe easily doubles for an 8 to 10 litre batch, or you can use 6 litres of milk by just adjusting the rennet amount to be roughly 1/4 + 1/8th of a tablet.

Variation: Caraway Havarti or caraway Gouda
A the start of the recipe, boil ¼ to ½ teaspoon caraway seeds in a small amount of water. Add the water with the kefir, and mix the seeds into the curds right before pressing.

Variation: Cool water Havarti
Remove whey, as you would for Gouda, but replace with water at 30°C (86°F).

Gently heat the pot over the course of half an hour to 38°C (100°F) using the stove or a hot water bath, until the curds have shrunk and developed a slightly springy texture, then finish the cheese as you would for hot water Havarti and Gouda.

Quick-glance method for experienced cheesemakers:
Culture at 32°C (90°F) for 30 to 45 minutes.
Rennet 30 to 45 minutes.
Cut 1.5cm (½") curds.
Rest 10 minutes, stir 5 minutes.
Remove 1 litre (1 quart) whey, slowly replace with water at 70°C (158°F).
When curds feel ready, put in mould and press with jar 20 minutes.
Flip, press with larger jar 3 to 8 hours.
Salt with 1 tablespoon salt.

All about Alpine cheese and mountain cheese

Alpine cheeses, sometimes known as Swiss cheese or mountain cheese, were created in areas around the Alps, where the dairy herds would move higher and higher up the mountains as the snow melted, being nourished by a range of herbs growing on rich glacial soils.

The cheeses were made every day, from fresh raw milk, not far from where the animals were grazing, where the dairy herders made cheese in simple huts. Often these huts did not have an ideal place for aging cheese, and some of these cheeses would get warmer than ideal during aging, encouraging the natural bacteria in raw milk that produces eyes.

When a cheese is made from this raw lower fat summer milk (or skimmed milk), using the cooked curd process, it gives a slightly elastic texture to the cheese where the famous holes of Swiss cheese (also known as 'eyes') can readily form. When the cheese is then subjected to high temperatures during aging, certain natural bacteria in the raw milk become active, creating a distinct flavour, and developing the eyes in the cheese.

The size of the eyes is proportional to the size of the cheese wheel - the traditional huge wheels of Emmental have large eyes. Small batch cheeses have smaller eyes, and are just as satisfying to eat. If you have lots of milk, feel free to double or triple my recipe to get a larger cheese with larger eyes.

If you've only tasted the industrial version of this cheese and not liked it, you may find that a raw milk version is completely different. I find that the artificial eye-forming bacteria added to industrial cheeses gives an unpleasant taste, and I am personally not keen on the washed rinds added to these cheeses by some small-scale cheesemakers, but when the bacteria naturally present in the raw milk are active instead, it has a subtle and beautifully balanced flavour, and makes a superb cheese for fresh eating or using in recipes.

In some of these cheeses, such as Emmental, the eyes are encouraged by purposely giving the cheese a time at a higher temperature after the rind has formed. For other styles of these cheeses, the aging is all done at typical cheese cave temperatures, and a few eyes may form.

For home cheesemaking, I am open to happy surprises - in summer I age these cheeses in my normal cheese aging space, it sometimes gets hotter than ideal and I end up with lots of lovely eyes, at colder times of year there are less eyes. Always it is delicious.

Jarlsberg from Norway can be considered an alpine cheese in some ways (although it is from nowhere near the Alps), because of the eyes, and because the dairy herds were managed in similar ways. If you follow the recipe on the following page and eat it quite young, it will taste similar to Jarlsberg. If you want an even milder version, you can follow the cool water Havarti variation on page 98, using raw milk, and heating to 46°C (115°F) and then following the aging process for the Emmental option in the following recipe, to encourage eyes to form in the cheese. Once the eyes have formed in the cheese, Jarlsberg is usually eaten earlier than Emmental.

Gruyère and Emmental

Culturing time: 30-60 minutes
Rennetting time: 15-40 minutes
Stirring time: 65 minutes
First pressing: 30 minutes
Second pressing: 30 minutes
Third pressing: 6 to 12 hours

These beautiful cheeses are traditionally made with raw milk, which naturally contains the eye-forming bacteria. You can make this with pasteurised milk, and it will still taste good, but you probably won't get eyes unless you follow my instructions below for adding a bit of Alpine cheese during the culturing phase.

To encourage the eye-forming bacteria, these cheeses are best made with raw milk that is slightly lower in fat, such as summer milk, or partially skimmed milk. Made with any kind of high quality raw milk they are delicious. I make these cheeses all through the year.

Low salt content can encourage the eye-forming bacteria, so if you suspect your cheese yield will be higher or lower than average, feel free to weigh your pressed cheese and add 1 to 1½ teaspoons salt per 200g (7oz) cheese to get the correct amount.

Ingredients
5 to 6 litres (6 quarts) non-homogenised milk, preferably raw

80ml (1/3 cup) milk kefir, viili, fresh whey, or yoghurt

Optional small piece of Gruyère or Emmental*

1/2 rennet tablet, 1/16 teaspoon powdered rennet, or 1/2 teaspoon liquid rennet

Additive-free salt

Equipment
Pot with at least 6 litre (6 quart) capacity
Spoon
Knife for cutting curds
Cheesecloth
800g (5" wide) cheese mould with follower

Method

1. Culture
Gently heat your milk to a lukewarm temperature of around 32°C (90°F). Thoroughly mix through the kefir, and leave it to culture for 30 to 60 minutes.

At this time, if you are concerned that your milk won't produce eyes on its own and desperately want eyes, you can also add part of a good alpine cheese, to bring some of the hole-making culture into your cheese, but this is optional. To do this, use a very fine cheesegrater to gently sprinkle your milk with cheese 'dust', or you can soak the piece of cheese overnight in a small amount of milk, and then remove the cheese, adding the cheese-cultured milk to the recipe with the kefir. If you want to do this, make sure that the cheese you get is very fresh and doesn't have preservatives added. I skip this step and just use raw milk – sometimes I end up with more eyes, and sometimes less.

2. Rennet
Dissolve the rennet in a quarter cup of water, stir it constantly and

then pour it over the milk. Quickly and thoroughly mix it through all the milk for a minute or two in an up and down motion, then leave it to sit until there is a clean break in the curd. If you've used very fresh milk, this should only take around 15 minutes; if the milk is older then it may take longer.

3. Cut curds
Cut the curds into small cubes, around 5mm (¼") in size. A large balloon whisk can be a good tool for this.

4. Heat and stir
Slowly heat the curds to 46°C (115°F) to 49°C (120°F) over at least 35 minutes while stirring often. The curds should shrink and get firmer.

Test your curds for readiness: when the curds are ready they will bind together when you squeeze a handful of them. Do the readiness test on page 50 to determine whether they are ready. If they are ready right away, then proceed to the next step, if not, then just keep holding them at 49°C (120°F) and stirring until they are ready.

5. Press
Allow the curds to settle, and pour off most of the whey. Line your cheese mould with cheesecloth and put the rest of the curds in here. Fold the cheesecloth over the top, cover with the follower, and press with a 1 litre (1 quart) jar filled with water for half an hour.

Remove the cheese from the mould and cloth, flip it over, rewrap, and then press from the other side with the same weight for another half an hour.

Remove the cheese, unwrap, flip and rewrap, press with the same weight or slightly more for 6 to 12 hours.

6. Salt
Remove the cheese from the cloth, rub 2 to 3 teaspoons unrefined salt over the surface of the cheese, and leave it to dry in a cool, airy place for 24 to 48 hours, to begin developing a rind.

Simple aging process:
Once the rind has formed, move the cheese to your usual aging space.

As the cheese ages, check on it once a week and flip it, rubbing the rind with a clean dry cloth or some salt if there are any unwanted moulds on it.

Optional warm aging instructions, to encourage more eyes if your cheese cave is cold:
After a few days, once the rind has formed, move your cheese to a place with a temperature of around 16-22°C (61-72°F) with fairly high humidity (a closed container can be used to increase humidity). Age it there for one to four weeks, wiping the cheese with a brine-soaked cloth and turning it over each day, making sure it's on a dry surface each time. A raw milk cheese should expand during this time, giving a rounded barrel-like look to the sides of the wheel.

Once the cheese has expanded (or you've waited long enough), bring the cheese back to the usual cheese cave conditions and age for at least another week, or for several months.

As the cheese ages, check on it once a week, rubbing the rind with some salt or a clean dry cloth around once a week.

When to eat:
Both methods of aging will create cheeses that develop more flavour as they age. Small batches can be eaten quite young, at around one month, when it will be mild and tasty, similar to Jarlsberg. Small batch Alpine cheeses will keep developing more flavour and continuing to dry out, for several months longer.

If you want to slow the drying out, feel free to store them immersed in sifted wood ash or wrapped in parchment baking paper after the first couple of months.

Bloomy white rind cheeses

Success with white bloomy rinded cheeses without packaged cultures will depend on what flora is present in the milk and the cheesemaking environment. I have tried to make bloomy rinded cheese in the past when my goats were eating mostly lucerne without success - I followed the recipe exactly, which told me that the raw milk and the natural culture I was using would already have enough fungus to culture the surface. I gave the cheese all the right conditions to mature, but the white rind just did not grow.

Now that my goats are eating a diet based on trees (mostly white maple, dogwood, and acacias at the time of writing this) white rinded cheeses seem to make themselves. Some quark sitting in a switched-off fridge that I was waiting to use in a cheesecake grew a perfect coating on the top and had the familiar mushroom-like scent of Camembert. An attempt at an alpine cheese that was stuck to the cheesecloth and abandoned on the kitchen bench for a couple of days was unwrapped to reveal a pleasant surprise of the bloomy white aroma and white fuzzy bits on it, the texture was a bit strange to eat it as-is, but when it was melted it reminded me of Brie melting on top of toast. Natural cheesemaking brings all kinds of surprises.

To encourage white rinds to grow you can bring some Camembert or Brie in from the grocery shop and put it next to the cheese that you want the white rind to grow on. You can also gently blow at the surface on the Camembert in the direction of your cheese, to help spread the spores, or add some of the rind to your milk during the culturing process, removing it before the rennet is added. Placing a storebought bloomy cheese directly on a wooden aging surface will bring white mould spores onto the aging surface that your cheeses will can pick up. It can be worth experimenting first with aging some chèvre or another small batch of cheese without bringing in any Camembert from the shop, just to see if your milk, culture, and aging space will already grow the right fungus without any effort.

To further encourage the growth of white moulds, use vinegar and salt to clean your aging surfaces, as this discourages unwanted moulds.

White fungus wants to grow in humid conditions. If your cheese cave is a bit lower in humidity, having a separate plastic box that you can use at first for getting the fungus growing will help. Washing the rind of the cheese every day or two for the first week using a mixture of whey and salt will also help to increase the humidity and discourage competing moulds from developing, but this step is not always necessary if the humidity is already naturally high. Be careful not to wash your cheese for too long (especially for small cheeses), or it may start developing orange washed rind bacteria, which are edible but are not to everyone's taste. The aim of the washing is to increase the humidity to favour the growth of white moulds, not to have the cheese surface constantly wet.

In France it is common for raw milk bloomy white cheeses to have some other moulds on the surface. If your bloomy white cheese ends up with some other moulds, it may not look like the pristine-looking industrial Brie we find at the shops, but as long as the moulds are edible, there is nothing to worry about – simply enjoy your delicious natural cheese. My bloomy white cheeses often end up spotted with blue cheese moulds - it still tastes like white mould cheese, but just looks different.

Moulds often work in succession, with the white moulds appearing first, some of these turning blue with age, before other moulds begin to colonise the cheese surface.

Bloomy white cheeses made without any added cultures are more often dominated by the wrinkly geotrichum fungus rather than the fluffy penicillium fungus that we're familiar with from industrial bloomy cheeses. The taste of these two moulds is similar, they just have a different appearance.

Optimum aging process for all bloomy rind cheeses

If you're concerned about not having high enough humidity to grow the white moulds, start by saving some of the whey from your cheese in a jar – strain it through cheesecloth to make sure the whey that you're using is clear green or yellow in colour and not milky. Add around 2 teaspoons salt to 1 cup (240ml) of whey. If you're not sure if your milk and aging environment has enough of the white mould in it, add a small piece of rind from a bloomy white cheese to this salty whey and leave it to soak.

If you wish to wrap your cheese in alcohol-soaked leaves to finish aging, soak leaves such as chestnut, walnut, maple, grape, or nettle in whiskey or brandy for a week or more.

Once your cheese is out of its form, salt the surface of your cheese, place it somewhere with plenty of airflow, and allow it to develop a rind for a day or two, as you would for any natural rind cheese. If you're sprinkling your cheese with ash, add this while the surface is still slightly damp. When it's ready for the next stage the cheese surface should feel dry to the touch. Once this dry stage is reached, wipe the surface of the cheese with a cloth dipped in the salty whey mixture and place the cheese in a high humidity environment such as a plastic box, ideally at around 10-13°C (50-55°F).

Turn the cheese every day for a week, wiping it every second day with more of the salty whey if the cheese surface looks dry. Continue to age in the high humidity place until a dusting of white fungus covers the whole surface of the cheese, then ideally move to a much colder place – around 3°C (37°F) is best, but typical cheese cave conditions will work too. If the place you are moving your cheese to is dry, wrap your cheese first in parchment baking paper, beeswax wrap, or non-toxic leaves to trap humidity close to the surface and encourage the white moulds. The cheese can now be eaten any time, or aged for several weeks.

Eaten earlier, there is less influence of the white fungus below the surface. Left to age, the surface fungus ripens the inside of the cheese as it develops more flavour and changes texture. Lactic curd aged chèvre bloomy rinds respond well to being eaten earlier, as they have plenty of of flavour of their own, whereas the fast coagulated cheeses such as Camembert and Brie are best left to age in their wrappings for at least a week or two to develop their full flavour.

Camembert and Brie

Ripening time: 1 hour
Rennetting time: 1 1/2 to 3 hours
First settling: 12 hours
Second settling: 12-24 hours

The original versions of these cheeses have many differences, mainly from the local conditions and what the cows graze on, as well as the size of the cheese, with Brie being larger and therefore taking longer to age and developing different flavours to Camembert. Outside of France, any locally made cheese labelled as Brie won't be made any differently to the same cheese called Camembert, especially if they're both made in small wheels. If you already make hard cheeses you will have a mould that can be used to make a Camembert, or maybe one that will make a cheese in between the sizes of Camembert (10cm or 4") or Brie (18cm or 7"). If you don't have one, you can have a look around the house to see what can be used to make either smaller wheels of Camembert, or a larger wheel of Brie. Clean wooden baskets might do the job, as might the basket of a salad spinner. You can punch holes in the sides of yoghurt buckets with straight sides, and plastic yoghurt jars with a straight section in the middle can be trimmed down to form open-ended moulds. Cylinder moulds with open bottoms will make the draining process easier, but with careful handling, basket-type moulds can be used as well. Moulds for large Bries are often made as two rings - both rings are stacked up while they are filled with curds, and once the curd has shrunk down to the level of the first ring, the top one is removed, making it easier to flip over.

This recipe will make two or three Camembert-sized cheeses, or one medium to large Brie cheese. If you don't have much milk, or if you want to try a smaller batch, you can easily halve this recipe and make one Camembert instead of two or three. For an easier recipe for a two litre batch of Camembert, see the next recipe.

Ingredients
4 litres (1 gallon) milk

60ml (1/4 cup) milk kefir, viili, or fresh whey

Optional small piece of Camembert or Brie rind

*1/8 to 1/4 rennet tablet, 1/64 to 1/32 teaspoon powdered rennet, or 1/8 to 1/4 teaspoon liquid rennet

Additive-free salt

Equipment
Pot with at least 4 litre (1 gallon) capacity

Spoon

Knife for cutting curds

Either 2 or 3 10-12cm (4-5") cheese moulds for Camembert, or an 18cm (7") mould for Brie

Method

1. Culture
Gently warm the milk to 32°C (90°F). Stir the kefir through the milk, add the small piece of Camembert rind now if you are using it. Leave to culture for an hour before removing the optional piece of cheese.

2. Rennet

Dissolve the rennet in ¼ cup water, stir it constantly and then pour it over the cultured milk. Quickly and thoroughly mix it through all the milk for a minute or two in an up and down motion, then leave it to sit for an hour and a half, or as long as three hours. The curd will have reached the clean break point much earlier than this, but we leave it for longer to develop the curd and acidity without stirring it.

3. Cut curds and drain

Cut the curd into 5cm (2") cubes if making Brie, 2cm (1") curds if making Camembert. Leave to rest for five minutes, to encourage the whey to separate, then ladle directly into the moulds. If there is any extra curd left, leave the moulds to settle for half an hour and then top them up with the extra curds. Keep some of the whey for making a brine to wipe the cheeses with.

Make the brine by combining 2 teaspoons salt with 240ml (1 cup) of whey and set it aside until later.

Leave the cheese to drain in the mould for 12 hours. It should be reduced in volume by half or more. Carefully flip the cheese over, returning it to the mould for another 12 or 24 hours, or until the cheese is firm enough to keep its shape. The draining process will be most successful at a fairly warm room temperature (around 21°C or 70°F).

4. Salt

Sprinkle the surface of the cheese with salt, around 1 tablespoon in total for a four litre (1 gallon) batch, then leave in a cool, airy place, until the surface appears dry; this should take around 24 hours. Flip the cheese over a couple of times during this process, moving it to a dry surface each time.

5. Age

Once the cheese is dry, age it in a high humidity space at the normal cheese cave temperature. If the humidity of your cheese cave is on the low side or if you have any doubts, feel free to start aging it in a plastic box with the lid ajar, and if you are still concerned about low humidity, for the first week of aging, wipe the surface of the cheese every second day with the salted whey brine, this will help to increase the humidity to encourage the white fungus to grow, while discouraging other blooms on the rind.

Once the first week has passed, stop washing the rind and carefully flip your cheese over twice a week, transferring to a dry surface each time. Continue doing this for three weeks, or until the cheese has a coat of white fungus. If any fungus other than the white or blue ones are growing, you may need to salt the surface of the cheese.

Once your cheese is coated in white fungus, you can wrap your cheeses in beeswax wrap or parchment baking paper (or you can use edible leaves such as grape leaves), and continue to age the cheese at a lower temperature such as in a fridge (or continue with cheese cave aging). Camembert will be ready after a month in the fridge, Brie in two months; both these cheeses will ripen more quickly at cheese cave temperatures and can be eaten earlier.

*Note:

The rennet amount for this cheese depends on your goals, your milk, and on the equipment that you're using. If you're using hard cheese forms to make this cheese, use a standard dose of rennet such as ¼ tablet, as it will make for a firmer cheese that is easier to get out of the mould without breaking. For bottomless moulds, you can get away with using less rennet, and usually it is best for this style of cheese to use slightly too little rennet rather than slightly too much. If you suspect your milk is low in solids, use the smaller amount of rennet, if your milk is high in solids, use the higher amount.

Simplified Small Batch Jar-Cultured Camembert

Rennetting time: 3 to 6 hours
First settling: 12 hours
Second settling: 12-24 hours

Ingredients
2 litres (2 quarts) milk

2 tablespoons (30ml) milk kefir, viili, or fresh whey

Optional small piece of Camembert or Brie rind

*1/16 to 1/8 rennet tablet, 1/128 teaspoon to 1/64 teaspoon powdered rennet, or 1/16 to 1/8 teaspoon liquid rennet

Additive-free salt

Equipment
2 litre (2 quart) glass jar

Knife for cutting curds

One 10 to 12cm (4-5") cheese mould, or several smaller ones

I created this recipe after making chèvre in a jar many times and wondering how that would work for other cheeses. Culturing cheese in a jar really simplifies the process when you raise your own dairy animals – just strain their fresh warm milk into the jar straight after milking, add your culture and rennet, and the cheese just makes itself.

The finishing and aging process beyond that is identical to the Brie recipe above.

Method
1. Culture and rennet
Start with milk at anywhere between 21°C and 32°C (70°F to 90°F) and place it in a clean 2 litre (half gallon) jar, leaving some space up the top for the culture and rennet. Mix through 2 tablespoons of kefir.

Dilute the rennet in around a quarter cup of water and pour this into the jar. Shake the jar slowly upside down and back up again a few times, to distribute the rennet, then leave, undisturbed for 3 to 6 hours, until separated into curds and whey. If you're culturing at the higher temperature, this may only take an hour, if this happens, just make sure to leave it for at least three hours in total, as this helps develop the acidity in the curd without stirring.

2. Cut curds and drain
Carefully cut the curd into one inch strips using a butter knife or other non-sharp knife. Leave to rest for at least five minutes to encourage the whey to separate. Place a cheese mould around 12cm (5") in diameter, and 13.5cm (5¼ inches) high into a bowl to catch the whey, and then gently pour the curds and whey from the jar into the mould. If the curds don't fit at first, leave it to settle for half an hour and then top it up with the remaining curds.

Remove the mould from the bowl and set it aside in a warm place (around 21°C/70°F) to drain for 12 hours. Pour the whey from the bowl into a jar – there should be around one cup (240ml). Add 2 teaspoons of salt to this and set it aside.

When the curd has drained for 12 hours, and has reduced by half or more, very carefully flip the cheese over and leave it to drain for another 12 hours, or up to 24 hours, until it's firmed up a bit and is more easily handled.

3. Salt
Sprinkle the surface of the cheese with 1½ teaspoons of salt, then leave in a cool, airy place, until the surface appears dry, this should take around 24 hours. Flip the cheese over a couple of times during this process, moving it to a dry surface each time.

4. Age
Once the cheese surface is dry, age it in a high humidity space at the normal cheese cave temperature. If the humidity of your cheese cave is on the low side or if you have any doubts, feel free to start aging it in a plastic box with the lid ajar, and if you are still concerned about low humidity, for the first week of aging, wipe the surface of the cheese every second day with the salted whey brine, this will help to increase the humidity to encourage the white fungus to grow, while discouraging other blooms on the rind.

Once the first week has passed, stop washing the rind and carefully flip your cheese over twice a week, transferring to a dry surface each time. Continue doing this for three weeks, or until the cheese has a coat of white fungus. If any fungus other than the white or blue ones are growing, you may need to salt the surface of the cheese.

Once your cheese is coated in white fungus, you can wrap your cheeses in beeswax wrap or parchment baking paper (or you can use edible leaves such as grape leaves), and continue to age the cheese at a lower temperature such as in a fridge, or at the usual cheese cave temperature. Camembert will ripen more quickly at cheese cave temperatures and can be eaten earlier, or can be slowly aged in the fridge for several weeks.

*Note: use the lower amount of rennet if you're using an open-ended mould or your milk is low in solids. Use more rennet if you're using a hard cheese mould or your milk is high in solids.

Quick-glance method for experienced cheesemakers:
Culture and rennet at 32°C (90°F) for 3 hours.
Cut into 2.5cm (1") strips.
Place in unlined cheese mould, reserving 1 cup (240ml) whey.
Drain for 12 hours.
Flip and drain for 12 to 24 hours.
Salt with 1½ teaspoons salt.

Blue cheeses

Any cheese can become a blue vein cheese by introducing it to the penicillium roqueforti mould, either from other blue cheeses, or from naturally present spores in the cheese aging space, and offering it the right conditions to grow.

On a blue vein cheese, at first a blue rind is encouraged to form, and then holes are poked through the cheese, to get the blue fungus on the rind to colonise holes in the cheese. In this way, you can take any cheese recipe and turn it into a blue cheese.

Blue cheeses are usually not pressed, in order to have more gaps in the cheese for the blue fungus to grow. To help the cheese to press under its own weight, choose a cheese mould that is tall but not too wide - your curds should fill up to the very top of the mould at first, so that the weight of the tall cheese will help it to press. As with any cheese, observation is key, and if your blue cheese is not sticking together under its own weight, feel free to add some weight. The curds can be salted and partly drained before being put in the mould; this dries out the curd, making for a cheese that can be aged for a longer time and develop more flavour.

Blue cheeses need careful handling, and if the rind appears crumbly after draining in the mould, it can be smoothed over with the back of a tablespoon heated in hot water. If your blue cheese is extremely fragile and looks like it wants to crumble to bits after being removed and salted, you can wrap a sushi mat around its edges and tie it firmly, to support the sides while still allowing it to breathe as it ages.

Blue cheese prefers quite high humidity, and you may find that when working with less-than-ideal cheese aging spaces, the blue moulds will thrive at certain times of year and not grow during the driest times of year. There are tricks that can be done to increase humidity, such as using a plastic box as described in the recipes for bloomy white cheeses, but for the most part I prefer to work with nature and accept that blue cheeses just don't do well in summer here.

Introducing blue cheese moulds

Blue moulds are probably already in your cheese aging space. If you aren't sure and want to be certain that blue moulds will outnumber the unwanted moulds in your blue cheeses, you can begin your blue cheese recipes by extracting blue fungus from another piece of cheese. To do this, start with a wedge of cheese that has a good amount of blue on it. Choose a cheese that you know hasn't been treated with preservatives, and for best results, find one that has been freshly cut. Carefully slice off an outside slice of this, to expose a fresh side of cheese that no person or wrapper has ever touched. Use a spoon or knife to dig out a piece of this fresh side of cheese, choosing a piece that has plenty of blue mould on it, a small piece around the size of an almond is fine. Take the piece of cheese and steep it in some water, breaking up the blue bits as much as you can to get them mixed into the water. Strain this water into the milk when you're adding the culture, then follow the rest of the recipe.

Blue moulds can be quite aggressive at certain times of year, so if you are making bloomy white cheeses and want them to be white, try to find a way to separate these from the blue cheeses as much as possible. If you need to rub or scrape your blue cheeses, move them to a different area to do this, to help prevent blue mould spores from floating around.

How to make a Gorgonzola-style blue cheese

• Make a triple or quadruple batch of the Feta recipe on page 90, following it until the curds are drained in the cheesecloth, optionally following the directions on page 110 to add some blue moulds when the culture is added.

Try to keep the temperature as close to 21°C (70°F) as possible during draining - in the following steps we are trying to encourage blue cheese to press under its own weight, but it will struggle to do this in cold temperatures.

An open-ended mould will make the flipping process easier and less likely to need additional weight.

• Drain curds in the cheesecloth without salting for an hour.

• Break curds into pieces roughly an inch in size, mix through 1 tablespoon salt before lightly pressing into a small batch hard cheese form or open cylinder mould and leaving to rest without any weight for 20 minutes.

• Carefully flip - if it's all a big mess and crumbles completely to pieces, add roughly 1kg (2 pounds) of weight for the second pressing.

• Press for 24 hours, flipping your cheese every now and then during this time, adding extra weight only if it is needed.

• Remove cheese from the form, leave in a cool airy place for two or three days, or until a rind has started to form.

• Age in high humidity conditions similar to bloomy white rinds for two or three weeks, until some blue fungus is showing on the surface.

• Once the surface has blue moulds, poke holes from the sides into the middle of the cheese with a sterilised metal skewer or knitting needle and continue to age in high humidity conditions for at least one month.

Cheddar

Cheddar cheese is often one of the first cheeses a new cheesemaker will aspire to make. Pretty much everyone is familiar with the mass-produced style of this cheese and can find a place for it in cheese sandwiches, grilled cheese, and many other dishes.

Cheddar is one of the last cheeses I'll write about in this book, for the reasons that it's more complicated to make than other cheeses, needs a cheese press, and many of the places that we find on the table for a slice of industrial Cheddar can readily be filled with cheeses that are easier to make.

Real Cheddar, aged in cloth, is a completely different cheese to the industrial Cheddar aged in plastic that we're most familiar with. Caerphilly is made in a similar way to Cheddar, but aged at high humidity with a natural rind, to bring some surface-ripening elements into the cheese.

Cheddar cheese originated in a time and place where there were a lot of cows to be milked, and a lot of milk that needed to be preserved. The Cheddaring, milling, curd salting, and heavy pressing processes make for a cheese that starts out quite dry and doesn't need much shelf space for aging, and the clothbinding means it doesn't need as much rind care as a natural rind cheese. The Cheddar style of cheesemaking can yield large wheels of cheese that will keep (and improve) over a year or more of aging. For small batches, I think anywhere between six weeks to nine months of aging is ideal, and this suits the seasonal cheesemaking cycle, preserving the summer and autumn milk abundance for the winter and spring.

Making real Cheddar cheese is not something I do every day - it is a slow process that is ideally suited to more milk than the cheeses in this book, but it can be a rewarding cheese to make every now and then. I find there is something meditative in hovering close to the stove on a rainy day, gently flipping the slabs of cheddar curds as they become firm and acidic. There's no need to be there the whole time – this process can be done every five minutes, just like the stirring process of any hard cheese. Please feel free to double or triple the following recipe if you have enough milk to do this, and your Cheddar will be better for it. I have also successfully made Cheddars from four litres (1 gallon) of high-solids winter goat milk.

Traditional Cheddar is covered in lard or ghee then wrapped in cloth, to stop the surface ripening bacteria from having an effect on the cheese, while still allowing the cheese to 'breathe' more than it would if it were covered in wax or plastic, making for a cheese that is ripened from the inside out to bring out different flavours to natural-rinded cheese. There is a noticeable difference between Cheddars that have been ripened in cloth and Cheddars from the same cheesery that are ripened in wax or plastic – the cloth-ripened ones have a better flavour and a slightly drier texture.

Cheddar can also be made with a natural rind, which when aged in humid conditions turns out similar to Welsh Caerphilly cheese – to do this just ignore the clothbinding instructions and treat your Cheddar as you would any natural rind hard cheese, preferably aging in high humidity conditions, as you would for bloomy rind cheeses.

Traditional Cheddar and Caerphilly

Method

1. Culture
Gently heat your milk to a lukewarm temperature of around 31°C (88°F). Thoroughly mix through the kefir, and leave it to ripen for 40 minutes.

2. Rennet
Dissolve the rennet in a quarter cup of water, stir it constantly and then pour it over the milk. Quickly and thoroughly mix it through all the milk for a minute or two in an up and down motion, then leave it to sit for around 30 minutes, until there is a clean break in the curd.

3. Cut curds, heat, and stir
Cut the curds into 1cm (1/2") cubes.

Slowly heat the curds to 39°C (102°F) over 45 minutes while stirring often. The curds should shrink to around the size of peas.

Keep the temperature at 39°C (102°F) for around 45 minutes, while stirring gently and frequently. When the curds are ready for the next step they will feel springy and will stick together when you do the readiness test with your hands (page 50).

4. Drain whey and make curds into slab
Allow the curds to settle, and pour off as much whey as possible. Drain the rest of the whey from the curds in a cheesecloth-lined colander.

Keep the curds warm and use the cheesecloth to gently bring the warm curds together into a single slab. Allow the slab to rest for around 10 minutes, for the curds to knit together.

Ripening time: 40 minutes
Rennetting time: 30 minutes
Stirring time: 90 minutes
Cheddaring time: 30 minutes
First pressing: 30 minutes
Second pressing: 30 minutes
Third pressing: 12 hours

Ingredients
6 litres (6 quarts) milk*

1/3 cup milk kefir, viili, or fresh whey*

1/3 a rennet tablet, 1/24 teaspoon powdered rennet, or 1/3 teaspoon liquid rennet*

Roughly 1 1/2 tablespoons additive-free salt

Lard or ghee, for optional clothbinding

Equipment
Pot with at least 6 litre (6 quart) capacity
Spoon
Knife for cutting curds
Cheesecloth and colander
800g (5" wide) cheese mould with follower
Cheese press
Optional cheesecloth, for clothbinding

5. Cheddaring
Cut the slab into several slices around 5cm (2") thick. Stack as many pieces as will go on top of each other without toppling over. You can cut the slabs in half to make smaller pieces to work with if you want.

Move the bottom slab to the top constantly (or as often as you can), to allow all the slabs to evenly press under their own weight while the acidity increases.

Make sure to keep the curds warm during this time, ideally between 32°C and 39°C (90°F and 102°F). You don't need to be there constantly for this, but moving the slabs around as often as you can (at least every five minutes) will make for a better cheese. If they are left for too long they will start knitting together, so try to move them often.

The curds will be ready when they have a strong rubbery texture, similar to a cooked chicken breast. This will usually take around 30 to 40 minutes.

6. Mill and salt
For best results, weigh the curds and add in 2.5% of the curd weight in unrefined salt. Break the curds up into pieces no bigger than an inch (2.5cm), add the salt, stir to combine, and leave to sit for 10 minutes while keeping the temperature warm to expel more whey.

7. Press
Put the salted curds into a cheese mould lined with cheesecloth, place in the cheese press, and press at half the maximum pressure for half an hour.

Remove the cheese, flip, and rewrap, then press for another half an hour at the same pressure.

Remove the cheese, flip, and rewrap, then press at the maximum amount of pressure for up to 12 hours.

8. Airing
Remove the cheese from the mould and allow it to dry in an airy place for a day or two, flipping it every so often, placing it on a dry place each time. Cheddar tends to be much drier than other cheeses for this stage.

9. Optional clothbinding
Bind your cheese in cloth by cutting four pieces of cheesecloth that will fit over the top and bottom of the cheese with an inch of excess cloth to go around the sides, also prepare two rectangles of cheesecloth to bind the side of the cheese.

Smear lard or ghee on the top of the cheese, press one piece of cheesecloth on this, smear or brush more lard where the excess cloth needs to stick on the sides, and press the rest of the cheesecloth into this. Cover the cheesecloth with more lard, and stick the second piece of cheesecloth over the top of this. Flip the cheese over and repeat for the other side, then cover the sides of the cheese with lard. Place one piece of cheesecloth around the sides, smear that with lard, and finish with the second rectangle of cloth.

10. Age
Age Cheddar for at least four weeks in a cheese cave. Some people prefer milder Cheddars aged for the minimum time, others prefer 6 months of aging. After 12 months Cheddar has a sharper flavour which some people prefer, and it can be aged even longer than this if you have a very large cheddar. If any mould develops on the cheesecloth during aging, wipe it off with some vinegar.

Caerphilly is generally eaten younger than Cheddar. 1 to 3 months of aging in humid cheese cave conditions with a natural rind is ideal.

Notes and variations:
*If you're using high solids winter milk, you can get away with making a smaller batch with just one gallon (4 litres) of milk - simply reduce the amount of rennet and culture accordingly.

Parmesan-style grating cheese

Some people reading this book may be wondering "where is the Parmesan recipe?!"

Parmesan is one of those well-known cheeses that many people are used to using in cooking, so it makes sense to be looking for a homemade version if you're making your own cheeses.

Many hard cheeses made in small batches will turn into something resembling Parmesan after several months, especially when they've been made with lower fat summer milk. The small wheel size means that they age and dry out faster.

Traditional Parmesan is made in very large batches and aged for a long time. It can be aged for two years because the wheels are huge. Parmesan is typically used in dishes where any hard cheese could be used instead, so as a small batch cheesemaker, I don't see the sense in making it.

Tomme (page 94) aged for five months or longer is my favourite for a dry grating cheese on top of pasta and other dishes where Parmesan would normally be called for. Younger tomme can also be very pleasant used in this way too.

It can be surprising to take cheeses that aren't at all similar to Parmesan and use them in place of Parmesan in recipes, but I think often when we are looking for Parmesan, we are looking for "flavoursome dry cheese", and any natural rind hard cheese can work in its place, especially if it has been aged for several months.

Basic guidelines for creating your own Parmesan-style cheese from a small batch:

• For best results, use raw milk.

• Skim some of the cream off, if using cows milk. For goats milk, use summer milk.

• Use a thermophilic-friendly starter culture such as yoghurt or kefir.

• Cut the curds very small, preferably with a whisk shortly after clean break, as you would for Alpine cheeses.

• Stir curds at the usual temperature for 25 minutes, then go through a cooked curd process as you would for Alpine cheese, slowly heating up to 52°C (125°F).

• Use a cheese press.

• Salt the surface with slightly more salt than usual: use around 2.5 to 3 teaspoons for every 200g (7oz) of cheese.

• Age at around 18°C (64°F), either at regular cheese cave humidity or lower-than-ideal humidity.

• Rub your cheese rind with olive oil to discourage moulds.

Whey ricotta

The vinegar-curdled ricotta recipe earlier in this book (page 72) is not considered to be real ricotta by some ricotta purists. Real ricotta is cultured cheese whey that is 're-cooked' by heating to a high temperature. It is sweeter, more delicate, with a lovely depth of flavour from the cultured milk.

To make whey ricotta, simply put a pot of whey leftover from a cultured and rennetted cheese on the stove, uncovered, and heat until clouds of ricotta form on the surface. Keep it warm (not boiling) for a further 20 minutes, and then gently use a slotted spoon to skim the lovely fluffy ricotta off the surface.

The yield is much lower compared to the vinegar-curdled milk version. To increase the yield slightly you can add some milk or cream to the whey, but this is not something I bother with – when I want lots of ricotta for cooking, I just do the vinegar and milk version.

Whey ricotta can be added to all kinds of foods or served on the side, from desserts through to savoury pies and tarts. It can also be mixed into gjetost at the same time that you add the milk to increase the gjetost yield.

Heating whey on the stove, the first step towards making whey ricotta and gjetost.

Norwegian Whey Cheese (Gjetost)

This delicious cheese is known by several names such as mysost and brunost, which can be made from either cow or goat whey, or gjetost, which is always from goats whey. This cheese is more of a caramel than a cheese – the whey gets slowly condensed and forms a soft sliceable cheese or spread that is excellent on toast. Slightly savoury, slightly sweet, very satisfying to eat, the taste is hard to describe. Many recipes insist on constant stirring, but I've made it in a few different ways, including using a solar cooker and on the woodstove, and Leigh at 5 Acres And A Dream makes it in a slow cooker, so it definitely is possible to make this delicious cheese without constant stirring! Some recipes call for using a blender in the final stages, but I have found this to also be unnecessary.

The first stage can take quite a while – I keep the pot with the lid off on the hottest part of the woodstove and generally ignore it, moving it aside whenever I need the stove for other cooking. In this first stage, the whey is reducing in volume. The second stage is when the whey starts to get quite thick and begins to caramelise, this stage happens faster and needs more watching.

Whey cheese begins with using whey leftover from any of the recipes in this book for hard cheese, cultured mozzarella, feta, or blue cheese. Whey from added acid cheeses such as ricotta and fast mozzarella will not work, and the slowly-cultured cheeses such as chèvre, quark, and yoghurt cheese will be too acidic for gjetost.

The fresher your whey is when you begin, the better your whey cheese will be, so for best results, start making whey cheese as soon as you've got your cheese pressing. Even if your stove is slowing down for the night and won't be able to do much of the boiling, starting the gjetost as soon as possible by heating it to a boiling or almost boiling temperature will stop it from souring.

You will end up with around 500ml (2 cups) of whey cheese for every 5 litres (5 quarts) whey. Yields will vary depending on whether you're stirring the ricotta back in, whether you are adding milk or cream (and how much of it you add), seasonal variations, and how thick you want your gjetost to be.

How to make Gjetost or Mysost

Step 1: First start off boiling off the whey in your cheese pot. Bring it to the boil, then skim the white solids that collect on the top and set them aside until later. These solids are ricotta, and you can either use them separately, or add them back into the gjetost later. More solids will rise during the process, but ignore those ones, as long as you get the first ones, you'll be right, and sometimes in tiny batches I don't even get these ones and it still turns out fine.

Just keep simmering the pot with the lid off, observing plenty of steam coming off it. Gradually it will reduce in volume.

This stage can take a long time, but is pretty hands off. It can be done on a woodstove, a slow cooker set on high, or very slowly in a solar cooker.

Step 2: Once the whey has reduced by half or more and is starting to thicken, for best results transfer the whey to a heavy pot such as an enamelled cast iron one, add back in the reserved ricotta if you like, and allow it to simmer gently with the lid off while it develops colour and becomes thicker.

During this final process you can also add in some milk or cream if you wish. Cream is what is traditionally used, but if you only have milk on hand then that can be used instead. The purpose of adding this is to give a higher yield, a creamier taste and texture, and a firmer consistency to the gjetost, but it is not essential. For every litre (quart) of whey that you started with before the great boiling-off, add up to 1/3 of a cup (80ml) cream or milk; for example, if you started with four litres (1 gallon) of whey, add up to 1 1/3 cups (320ml) milk or cream.

As the whey thickens into whey cheese, keep an eye on it, reduce the temperature a little, and stir it every now and then to prevent it burning on the bottom. I usually do this stage on a cooler part of the woodstove, as doing this stage on high heat needs a lot more stirring and watching. For solar cooking, the edges of the pot can start to get overcooked while the insides are still very liquid during this stage, so make sure you are nearby to stir it every now and then as you would for a woodstove or slow cooker gjetost. Do the 'spoon test' as you would for chutney, picking up a wooden spoonful of whey cheese, running your finger horizontally through it, and seeing whether any of the gjetost drips onto that line.

You can also do the 'plate test' as you would for jam – place a small amount of your gjetost on a cold plate and wait until it's completely cooled – you will now have a better idea of its finished texture, whether it is too runny and not ready at all, a spread that is thick enough to be spread with a knife, or a solid, sliceable cheese.

The longer you reduce and stir it for, the thicker it will be. The colour will change from light tan for a spreadable goats whey gjetost and become darker the more it is reduced. Mysost from cows whey will start off a darker colour than gjetost, and can become quite dark when it is solid. For best results, do the plate test above rather than relying on colour alone to determine when your gjetost is ready.

Once your whey cheese has reduced enough, either spoon it into jars, or for very thick whey cheese, you can place it in traditional Norwegian wooden moulds with removable sides, or in silicone muffin cups or other silicone moulds.

Whey cheese can be kept at room temperature for a week or two, or for much longer in the fridge or larder. It can also be frozen for several months.

I serve gjetost on bread or toast, either on its own, with salted butter, or with some jam or fruit syrup on top.

Other dairy products

Kefir

To make real kefir, I recommend tracking down some milk kefir grains. These can be gained for free from people who make milk kefir themselves, or purchased online through shops that sell cultures. There is another form of kefir called water kefir, the grains for these have a different appearance to milk kefir, with milk kefir grains looking like tiny cauliflowers, and water kefir grains like translucent squares. Make sure you get the milk kefir grains to make this recipe.

To make milk kefir, add a teaspoon of freshly rinsed milk kefir grains to one cup of milk, leave it to ferment at room temperature for eight to twenty four hours. The fermenting time will depend on how active your grains are, the ratio of grains to milk, and the temperature.

After the kefir has fermented as much as you want it to, remove the kefir grains and rinse them with cold water, and then begin your new batch, or put them in a little bit of milk in the fridge to be stored for later. It's important to rinse kefir grains in this way in between batches, to avoid any off-flavours developing from overfermented milk that may have stuck to the kefir grains.

The taste of kefir is not for everyone. If you don't like the taste to begin with, try fermenting for a shorter amount of time or reducing (or increasing) the amount of grains used, using milk from a different animal, or adding a teaspoon of honey and a pinch of cinnamon to every cup of kefir for drinking.

You don't have to enjoy the taste of kefir to make cheese with it. Just make sure you have some fresh kefir without anything added to it for your cheesemaking if you want to use it as a starter. You'll only need around a quarter of a cup (60ml) of kefir for a hard cheese made from four litres (1 gallon) of milk, even less if you're making a small batch of soft cheese. You can store the kefir grains in the fridge in a small amount of milk; just rinse them and then begin a new batch of kefir 8 to 24 hours before you want to make cheese. If the kefir has been in the fridge for quite a while, it may need to be rinsed and fed a second time before it's ready to use.

The more frequently your kefir is fed, the more active it will be. If you find that your cheeses made with kefir are not culturing as quickly as they should, try feeding your kefir more frequently, keeping it around the same temperature that you'll be culturing your cheese.

If the temperature of your kitchen fluctuates a lot in winter, you may find that sometimes kefir can be very slow to culture and may need to culture for 48 hours before it's active enough for cheese. I keep mine near the stove in winter, allowing extra time for it to culture as the kitchen cools overnight.

Yoghurt

The thickness of yoghurt will vary depending on which animal's milk it's made from. Individual animals in a herd will make different yoghurt, although cows milk is usually pretty predictable for making beautiful creamy yoghurt. My first Toggenburg goats always made fairly thin yoghurt, the Saanen/Nubian cross that I looked after made the best thick yoghurt, and the pure Saanen yoghurt is somewhere in the middle of these. If you mix all your milk together you may get decent yoghurt, or you may not, so if you keep goats, it can be worth trying each goat's milk one by one to see which is the best. Winter milk also makes thicker yoghurt than summer milk. Feeding barley to animals will increase the thickness of their milk.

Yoghurt will be thicker if it is first heated above 82°C (180°F), and then left to cool to the culturing temperature. If you can heat it up slowly, or hold it at the goal temperature for half an hour, this will help to create thicker yoghurt. This changes the protein structures in the milk, to help create a thicker yoghurt. Although this ends up pasteurising the milk, the cultures added back in quickly colonise the milk with good bacteria and turn it into yoghurt.

The easiest kinds of yoghurt to make are room temperature cultures such as viili. These cultures work best at around 23°C (73°F).

For a yoghurt taste more similar to the kind that we might buy in the grocery shop, use some Greek yoghurt with live cultures and follow the instructions on the following page to help these thermophilic (heat loving) cultures to grow. Cultures that include acidophilus strains of bacteria are generally easier to manage at home than other Greek and Bulgarian yoghurt cultures.

Yoghurt of all kinds is best made at least once per week, to keep the culture fresh. It is worth keeping a small amount of yoghurt tucked away in the freezer, just in case your yoghurt gets contaminated or abandoned.

Viili and other room temperature yoghurts

To make viili, start with a jar around ¾ full of milk, then add a decent amount of of viili from a previous batch, put the lid on, and gently shake it a bit to mix it through. The right ratio is around 5 tablespoons (75ml) of viili to one quart or litre of milk but there's no need to be exact about it, just don't put too little in or the viili culture may not be able to multiply enough before the cultures already in the milk take over. If you only have a tiny amount of viili to begin with, just make a smaller batch and then make a bigger one once the small batch is finished.

If the yoghurt is not thick enough for your taste, you can ferment it for longer, until the whey separates, and then drain it through some cheesecloth as you would for chèvre until it's as thick as you'd like it to be.

In winter I used to put the viili on a warm (not hot) part of the wood stove and let the yoghurt gently warm up a bit (until the bottom of the jar feels nicely warm when put on the inside of the wrist), and then move it to a fairly warm part of the house to finish fermenting. Sometimes it needs a second or third go on the wood stove. In warmer weather (or warmer houses), normal room temperature is fine. 24 hours is usually all the time that's needed to culture the viili in warm weather, 48 hours is more realistic when it's cold.

You will need to track down some viili culture to make this yoghurt. I found mine on eBay. Cultures for Health also sell viili culture.

Greek and Bulgarian yoghurt

Heat the milk until it reaches 82°C (180°F) or higher, hold it at or above that temperature for half an hour, if possible, and then let it cool to around 40°C (104°F). Stir or shake through the yoghurt using around 5 tablespoons (75ml) of yoghurt for every quart (litre) of milk, and keep your yoghurt at 40°C (104°F) for the next six hours or more. Some ways of doing this are: fermenting it in an insulated food jar such as a thermos, or surrounding a normal jar with hot water in an esky or on the edge of a woodstove dying down for the night.

In real life, the temperature does tend to drop slightly over that time, so it's sometimes easier to start culturing it at a slightly higher temperature (up to 46°C or 115°F), and leave it culturing for twelve hours or more rather than six. Some of the helpful yoghurt bacteria will still be active in the lower temperatures, and the heat-loving bacteria will still have some time to grow during the earlier, warmer stages of culturing.

In winter I leave my yoghurt jar overnight in a pot of warm water on the edge of the woodstove as it cools down, and then refill the pot with warm tap water in the morning to give it more time to culture at high temperatures. I find that yoghurt tastes the best after around 18 hours of culturing in this way during winter.

For thick Greek yoghurt, allow your yoghurt to continue culturing at warm room temperature until the whey begins to separate. Pour it into cheesecloth and allow the curds to continue dripping whey until it's as thick as you'd like it to be, anywhere between two and twelve hours.

A few tips to get the thickest yoghurt

• Experiment with using milk from different animals or different sources. One of the goats here gives very creamy milk that makes excellent thick yoghurt, my other goats give milk that makes a thinner yoghurt. If I were mixing all the milk together I would not have noticed this. Full fat cows milk generally makes lovely thick yoghurt, and milk from a Jersey cow or other cow that gives extra creamy milk will make even thicker, lovelier yoghurt.

• You can evaporate some of the liquid out of the milk, by leaving the pot on the heat with the lid off once it's reached temperature – just observe the level of the milk you start off with, and then remove from the heat and allow the pot to cool once it's reduced by ¼ to ½.

• Once you get your milk heated to 82°C (180°F), holding it at or above that temperature for half an hour or so will help transform more of the protein, to make for a thicker yoghurt.

• If in doubt, add more yoghurt to start it off, rather than less. Some recipes advise using only two tablespoons for a litre (quart) of milk, but I always use 5 tablespoons and it doesn't hurt it, it just makes the milk get colonised more quickly while the temperature is warm.

• Make yoghurt often - the fresher your culture is, the more active it will be for colonising the next batch. I like to make yoghurt at least twice a week for this reason.

- To keep your yoghurt culture as active and pure as possible and avoid having to buy new culture, it's a good idea to keep everything as sterile as possible: heat and cool your milk in a pot with the lid on, heat-sterilise your jars and any spoons you'll be using, don't leave the jars open to the air any longer than you have to, and be very careful with any jar of yoghurt that you'll be using as a starter for your next batch - pour the yoghurt out rather than reaching in with a spoon (unless the spoon is heat sterilised). For even better results, make an extra smaller jar of yoghurt that you can use as your culture, and then it doesn't matter what happens to your jar of eating yoghurt. You can also store small jars of yoghurt in the freezer to use as a backup culture in case your regular one gets contaminated.

Sour cream and cultured butter

To make sour cream, thoroughly stir 1 tablespoon (15ml) kefir, viili, buttermilk, or crème fraîche into 1 cup (240ml) of pure cream in a jar. Cover with a lid and leave it to sit at around 22°C (72°C) for 12 to 24 hours, until it smells and tastes lightly cultured. Store in fridge or cellar conditions - it will thicken more as it cools down and sets.

To make butter, agitate the cream. There are many ways to do this. I use a large bowl and a whisk, as it allows me to make more butter at once than the shaking-the-jar method. It is slow work, but making it from soured cream makes it much tastier, and faster.

Other ways to agitate the cream include big old wooden paddle-churns, wooden plunger-type churns, small glass jar churns, and just shaking it in a plain jar. A food processor or blender will also do the job. All these methods take around the same time as the whisk method. It's important to only half-fill the butter-making container, as the cream expands a lot during the process.

Cream goes through a few stages when transforming into butter. The more sour the cream is, the more quickly it will transform. With non-soured cream it firsts behaves as if you are turning it into whipped cream, becoming softly whipped, then stiffly whipped, and then the cream will begin to separate into buttermilk and butter, with the butter becoming more and more yellow. Soured cream will often separate into butter and buttermilk very quickly, with no 'whipped cream' phases at all.

Once the butter has separated, squash it into a clump (or a few smaller clumps) and put it into a bowl of very cold water. Set the buttermilk aside for using in recipes. Knead the butter in the water to help get more of the buttermilk out (this will help it to keep for longer), then knead it in another change of cold water if you want to be extra thorough.

Knead a small sprinkle or two of salt into the butter if you wish (this also helps it to keep for longer), and then wrap the butter up in beeswax wrap or parchment baking paper, or squash it into jars.

Ghee (clarified butter)

Ghee is a way to preserve butter in warm weather without a fridge. To make ghee, first heat-sterilise a canning jar, and keep it warm in the oven. Keep it warm but not hot, until you're ready to pour the ghee.

Take unsalted butter and put in a pot (preferably cast iron) over medium-low heat. Allow it to simmer, uncovered. You will notice foam developing, this is the first stage. Observe the simmering butter, until you notice solids on the bottom of the pan (you might need to move the foam aside with a spoon every now and then to check) - this means that the milk solids have now clumped together and your ghee is ready to strain.

Waiting for the solids to form is a slow process. I do it when I'm pottering about in the kitchen and can keep an eye on it. There have been times when I've left the kitchen for a while and it's ended up overcooked - that is fine too, it just gets more of a caramelised taste and a brown colour rather than the bright yellow that perfectly-cooked ghee turns into once it's set.

Take the pot off the heat for five minutes or so - the ghee at this point is extremely hot, and if you pour it now it's likely to crack the jar.

Put a funnel and some cheesecloth on top of the warmed jar. Carefully pour the warm-hot ghee into the warm jar, put the lid on, and allow it to cool. If you want to increase its storage life, use a lid with a good seal, and flip the whole filled jar upside down for a minute or two.

Custard

Custard made from real cream is the best. It's also possible to make it from milk - just choose milk from your animal that gives the creamiest milk, and for best results, add in a little tapioca flour or gelatin to help thicken it.

Ingredients
- 2 cups (480ml) milk or whipping/pouring cream
- Optional 1 or 2 tablespoons tapioca flour (aka arrowroot starch) or a small amount of gelatin
- 1 or 2 tablespoons coconut sugar or honey
- A pinch of vanilla bean powder, or a teaspoon of vanilla extract
- 5 egg yolks

Method
Heat the milk up, stirring every so often, until it feels very hot and is about to boil.

While the milk is heating up, in a measuring jug or bowl, mix together the tapioca flour or gelatin, coconut sugar, vanilla bean powder and egg yolks until evenly combined.

Pour a little of the hot milk into the egg yolk mixture and mix until evenly combined, then add a bit more, mixing through again, and then add as much as will fit in the jug. Pour the mixture back into the saucepan, mixing thoroughly if there's any more milk left in there. Return to a low-medium heat and continue to heat up, while stirring, until thickened and hot. Serve hot, either on its own or as a side to steamed puddings, stewed fruit and crumbles, or serve it as a cold dessert.

No-Churn Ice Cream

Here's a way to make ice cream without any special machines or gadgets. A simple combination of cream, egg yolks, and honey forms a treat that can be served on its own, or on the side of your favourite desserts.

Ingredients
- 500ml (2 cups) whipping cream with around 35% fat content and no additives
- 85g (¼ cup) honey
- 4 fresh egg yolks
- optional 1 teaspoon vanilla powder or extract

Method
Whip the cream until peaks form. Heat the honey until bubbling, and allow it to bubble for two minutes.

Whisk the egg yolks and then add the honey in a thin stream, continuing to whisk it in to form a light bubbly mixture, and whisking for another two minutes. Mix through the vanilla, if using.

Carefully mix the cream into the honey and egg yolks, put in a container or individual moulds and freeze until solid.

This ice cream is best if allowed to sit for 5 minutes at room temperature before serving.

Appendix A:
Troubleshooting, and how to achieve the results you want

Cheesemaking troubleshooting

Help! I'm in the middle of making a cheese and I've unexpectedly had to leave it!
Depending on what stage of the cheese you're at, the approach is slightly different.

If you are just warming up the milk and haven't added culture or rennet yet, you could decide to make chèvre or soft cheese instead, as this is a very flexible cheese that you can come back to any time.

If you've just added the culture and will only be away for an hour or two, you can add the rennet right away, and add the culturing and rennetting time together before cutting the curds with a knife.

If you've just added the culture (or the rennet as well) and you have to leave, you can try and reduce the temperature to make it culture or rennet more slowly by putting the pot in a cold place, and picking up the rest of the cheesemaking recipe later on. This may end up creating an acidic cheese with raggedy curds that end up as a cultured mozzarella (see 'curds stuck to cheesecloth', page 130), or it may not, just be observant and make whatever cheese you can from it.

During the stirring phase, again, moving it to a colder place will help it to slow down the acidification and release of whey.

If you've had to leave the cheese for longer than expected during culturing, rennetting, or curd cutting, you can reduce acidity by using the washed curd technique (see the Havarti and Gouda recipe on page 98) to heat the curds and finish the cheese that way.

If you've just started the first pressing, have a peek and see if the curds hold together enough to flip and re-wrap early. If it doesn't, don't despair, just leave it on the first pressing and it will probably be fine.

If you've just drained your mozzarella and have to leave, the stretching can be left until later. If it's cultured mozzarella, keep it in a cold place until you're ready, to prevent further acidifying.

Help! I forgot about my cheese and it's been sitting there culturing or rennetting for too long!
Speed the rest of the cheese process up to quickly finish the cheese while minimising further acid buildup, and/or use the washed curd method to reduce the acidity.

Fresh curds have gassy bubbles
This is most noticeable in a slowly-cultured cheese such as chèvre. It is caused by contamination by gas-forming bacteria or yeasts that get a chance to multiply before the good bacteria can take over. I only make chèvre from the very freshest milk, adding the kefir and rennet quickly so that it gets a chance to culture with the desired bacteria before anything else can take over. How the milk is handled before cheesemaking can also make a difference - I am careful to heat-sterilise my milking bucket, straining cloth, and jars before use (see page 19), and to strain the milk as soon as possible.

Some individual animals can be more prone to carrying coliform bacteria than others, so if you keep dairy animals, it can be worth keeping each animal's milk separate and experiment with making small cheeses from each one, to pinpoint the source of contamination. Looking at how the animals have been kept can also help – observe where they go to sit down, and add fresh straw or woodchips to these places to help keep them clean.

Once when my cheeses consistently had these bubbles, I figured out that it was probably from the previous day's milk, and began my cheesemaking by low-temperature pasteurising the older milk at 63°C (145°F) for 30 minutes, and then adding the fresh raw milk to bring the temperature down.

For anyone who does not want to pasteurise at all, and is planning to make cheese the next day, one option is to add a tiny amount of kefir to the milk as soon as possible, and leave it in cool storage - this introduces beneficial bacteria that can take over before the gas-forming bacteria have a chance. If this is done, then the culturing time for the cheese should be removed from the recipe, so that the rennet is just added to the cultured milk right away. Careful observation will need to be made, and if too much acid is developing and the curd is sticking to the cheesecloth, then you may need to use washed curd techniques to change the recipe next time.

Storing the previous day's milk as cold as possible will also help.

For chèvre, if you are trying all the above suggestions and are still having trouble, you can try coagulating at 16-17°C (62°F) instead of the recommended 22°C (72°F).

Curd hasn't set at all

If you've reached the point when it should be time to cut the curds, and there's no clean break, or it's not even set at all, first check the temperature of the milk; it may be that it is too cold. Gently warm it up to the correct temperature, if needed. If it still hasn't set after giving it a bit more time at the correct temperature, then add back in the same dose of rennet that you initially added and allow it some more time to set.

If the temperature has been warm enough but it still has not set, check your culture to make sure it has plenty of flavour – it could be that the cheese has not developed enough acidity to form curds with the rennet. Allowing more time will help in this case, as well as encouraging your starter to be more active (see the kefir recipe on page 120).

It could be that the rennet is losing its power and more needs to be used to get the same results. Observe this carefully and change your standard rennet dose accordingly.

To test rennet for effectiveness, see page 22.

Milk that is contaminated with antibiotic residues can make it more difficult for cultures to grow. Check your source of milk.

Check the water that you use for diluting the rennet. add a drop of non-raw vinegar if it is alkaline; if it is chlorinated, then either use a different water source, or allow your chlorinated water to stand out overnight uncovered to evaporate the chlorine. Also make sure the rennet is diluted only shortly before adding it to the milk – if left to stand in the water for too long, rennet will lose its effectiveness.

Soft cheese taking too long to drain
This is usually because the temperature is too cool. 22°C (71°F) is ideal. Open the cheesecloth up and stir the cheese around, scraping the cheesecloth to scrape off any 'skin' of dry curds that may have formed around the edges. Try to increase the temperature if you can, and give it another stir later on if it is still draining too slowly. Also look at the cheesecloth you are using – it may be too fine and you might want to track down something more loosely woven (see page 32 for my recommendations). If you've been draining at the ideal temperature using the best weave of cheesecloth and are still having trouble with this, experiment with using slightly more rennet next time and/or allowing more culturing time, ideally long enough so that the uncut curd is covered with a 1cm (½") layer of whey.

Having trouble keeping the cheese warm enough
During the culturing or rennetting stage, it can help to heat the milk slightly higher than the recipe says. If you heat to 34°C (93°F) or slightly higher instead of 32°C (90°F), then this will allow more room for the rennet to develop at the optimum temperature.

To keep the curds at the right temperature for as long as possible before pressing, you can place a large bowl underneath your cheese mould, and use this to catch the whey and surround the curds with warmth while you add them to the cheese mould in it, arrange the cheesecloth on top, and start the pressing.

If you suspect the room temperature will be too cold during the pressing phase, you can pour all the whey into glass jars, and snuggle this up around the pressing cheese to help keep it warm for longer. Jars of warm water will also do the same job. If your cheese recipe doesn't need a cheese press, feel free to press using a jar of warm whey or warm water.

Another strategy to keep the cheese warmer during the pressing phase is to make cooked curd cheeses, or just heat the cheese slightly higher than the recipe says, so that the curds are warmer when they go into the press and will stay warm for longer during the pressing phase.

During the pressing phase, the most important thing to remember is that what happens early on impacts the cheese more than what happens later. Keep the first pressing to 20 to 30 minutes and don't delay the flipping and re-wrapping, so that the cheese is pressing on its second side while it's still slightly warm from the cooking process.

If you're pressing your cheese with a jar of warm whey, tipping some of this out at the start of the second press and replacing it with very hot water will help bring the temperature back up, just make sure not to let the temperature in the jar get above 49°C (120°F).

Avoiding delay at every step will help to keep the curds warm – work quickly, especially once the whey is drained.

Soft cheese has a rubbery texture
This is usually because too much rennet has been added, or because the milk is low in fat. Next time try halving the amount of rennet – for liquid rennet, I dilute the tiniest drop that I can get in water, and often end up throwing out half the water or more. For powder and tablet rennet, it's easier to measure it out.

Sometimes the edges of the curd touching the cheesecloth will become a little rubbery as the cheese is draining. I just try to break these bits up as best I can when salt is added, mixing it in to the other curds to help hydrate it before continuing to drain.

More fat in the milk will make for a softer soft cheese, so if you have the rennet dose low enough and are still getting rubbery curd at certain times of year, consider adding some cream to your milk, or concentrating your soft cheese efforts for the times of year when there is naturally more fat in the milk.

Low cheese yield from the milk

There are a few different things that impact the yield of cheeses. The most important one is the age of the milk. While milk sits in storage, some of the protein changes from the soluble protein that we want in our cheese, into dissolved protein which ends up in the whey.

The diet of the animals will impact the amount of solids in the milk; feeding them barley is said to increase the cheese yield, although I have not noticed any difference in cheese yields between feeding barley and feeding oats. The time of year will change the cheese yield - animals give thicker milk at the start of lactation and in colder weather, and more watery milk in summer.

Milk made from animals with mastitis will give lower cheese yields.

I deal with the varying yields of cheeses by expecting seasonal variations in yield and being prepared for it, avoiding mastitis, and aiming to make cheese as quickly as possible after milking.

Curds not firm enough

Check that your curds are at the correct temperature for the recipe, and leave for a little longer. Cut carefully and stir carefully. If your curds are really delicate and you had planned to make a cheese that requires firm curds with lots of stirring, consider working with a different recipe that uses less stirring, and be very careful while you're stirring.

Observe the yield of curds to whey. If it appears that you have a lot of curds, it may be that you did not add enough rennet. Next time when working with milk in similar conditions, increase the rennet dose.

Some cheesemakers at some times of year will add small doses of calcium chloride to their cheese (add 5 minutes before rennetting) to help get the curds to set more firmly.

If you're raising your own milk animals, you may find that this happens if their feed is low in calcium. Consider giving your animals free-choice access to a salt lick containing calcium and phosphorus, as well as working to improve soil health and mineral content.

Mozzarella doesn't stretch

The ideal temperature and timing for stretching sometimes varies from batch to batch. Try keeping the curd in the salted whey for longer, as it sometimes takes a minute or two for it to soften. If that doesn't work, try heating the salted whey to a higher temperature. Check your curd frequently when adding it to the hot salted whey, as it can change from being not stretchy at all, to running off the spoon quite quickly. The stretchiness of mozzarella can also change through the milking season. The important thing to remember is that even if your mozzarella doesn't stretch, it will still make good pizza.

Curds stuck to cheesecloth

Be very careful as you remove the cheesecloth. You can try soaking it in warm whey at this point, to see if that will help. If this happens, it's good to remember for next time to soak the cheesecloth in warm whey for a few minutes in advance, as the change in the cloth pH makes it less likely for the curds to stick.

If this problem persists, it could be that your cheeses are turning out to be too acidic. Try making a washed curd cheese such as a Gouda or Havarti, or just following any cheese recipe, removing a quarter of the whey and replacing with water. You can also try adding the rennet at the same time as the culture, or making the process go more quickly.

Observe the curds – if they're ragged in appearance and stretch when exposed to high heat, then you've accidentally created a cultured mozzarella, and if you're flexible, you can just enjoy it as a cultured mozzarella instead of pressing it.

Another way that this can happen is when the cloth and cheese mould have been freshly boiled and have not cooled down enough yet, so the cheese is melting into the hot cloth. It's important to keep this in mind - I try to sterilise the cloth and mould as soon as the curd is cut, so that it has time to cool down even if the curds end up being ready sooner than expected.

Even if you don't sterilise your cheesecloth, always make sure it is damp, either with whey or with water, as this will also help to prevent sticking.

Flipping and re-wrapping more frequently can help, as can using less weight to press the cheese.

Hard cheese has a big dent in it, or is uneven on one side.

This happens if the cheesecloth hasn't been folded on top carefully enough. You can remedy this in your current cheese by flipping the cheese and giving it another pressing, this time first very carefully arranging the cheesecloth over the top folding over one side at a time to form a thin, even layer over the top of the cheese. If you end up with excess cloth, carefully fold it back on itself to form another thin even layer. See page 54 for pictures.

Aging troubleshooting

Hard cheese bulges at the sides in the early stages of aging
Sometimes this is from the eye-forming bacteria that we encourage in Alpine cheeses, other times the weight of the cheese combined with the moisture of the curds can cause the cheese to bulge on the sides during the early stages of aging. This is not always a bad thing, as it can create quite attractive shapes. To encourage it to bulge evenly, flip your cheese over often during the first few days of aging. If for some reason you really don't want any roundness to the rind, consider brining your cheese instead of dry salting, as the brine will help support the weight of the cheese during the earliest stage of aging, or dry salt your cheese and put it back in the mould without weights for another 12 hours, before airing as you normally would; this allows the cheese to further drain and begin firming up before it needs to support itself.

Hard cheese rind appears dry and cracked
The humidity may be too low in your aging space. Work on ways to increase the humidity. Also aim to put your curds in the mould early rather than too late, especially for cheeses with quite dry curds, such as Cheddar. Aim also to use as minimal weight as possible when pressing – just enough to get the curds to knit together and form a rind, and gradually increase the weight as needed.

Oiling the rind with olive oil may also help, or focusing on waxed, clothbound and brine-aged cheeses at the driest times of year may also help, see pages 64 and 88. After the first month of aging, a small batch hard cheese can be wrapped in parchment baking paper or buried in sifted wood ash, to help keep it from drying out too much in dry conditions.

Aged cheese is too crumbly
This is probably caused by acid being developed quickly. Acids dissolve the calcium in milk and transfer it to the whey rather than keeping it in the curds, a smaller amount of calcium left in the final cheese makes for a crumbly texture rather than an elastic one.

To make your cheeses less crumbly, you can try making a washed curd cheese such as Gouda or Havarti, or inventing your own cheese by replacing some of the whey with water, but not as much as in a washed curd cheese recipe. Reducing the amount of culture used, or using kefir that is only just cultured for 8 hours rather than longer can also help. Cooked curd techniques, as used in Alpine cheeses, also slows the development of acid.

The amount of calcium in milk will vary throughout the season, so you may find that at certain times of the year there is naturally less calcium in the milk, and the cheeses will be crumblier. If you are consistently having problems, looking into the animals diet and/or giving them access to a mineral lick that has both calcium and phosphorus in it may help.

Aged cheese tastes bitter
Cheeses often go through a bitter-tasting stage of aging - try leaving it to age for longer.

Be very careful when measuring rennet, and calcium chloride (if using); too much of either of these things can impact the flavour of the cheese.

Lots of holes in aging cheese

In many cheeses there will be some bubbles and openings from where curd has not knitted together, but during aging, when a cheese bulges at the top, and reveals a huge amount of holes when cut into (sometimes looking like a sponge), sometimes accompanied by cracks, there are a couple of different causes. In the first ten days of aging, this is caused by similar coliform bacteria and yeasts to the gassy bubbles in fresh curds. If the bulging happens later in aging, it is sometimes caused by clostridia bacteria, and sometimes by the propionic bacteria that is encouraged in Alpine cheeses.

For the bubbles forming in the early stages of aging, some sources say not to eat these cheeses at all, other sources say that they won't be great cheeses, but they are still edible. Some of my cheeses with this flaw have had a bad taste, but most have tasted fine, I've eaten them, and I'm still alive to tell the tale. What you do if you get this flaw in your cheeses is up to you.

For excessive bubbles forming between ten days and one year of aging, it's either propionic bacteria, or the c.butyricum strain of clostridia - neither of these are dangerous in any way.

Clostridia contamination is far more likely to occur if your milking animals have been fed silage. If you suspect clostridia, make sure you are not making cheese from silage-fed animals. Also, in future batches, weigh your cheese after pressing and measure out the correct amount of salt to use (see page 56). Cheddar and other cheeses that have their curds thoroughly salted before pressing are also less likely to have this flaw.

Aged cheese (or aging cheese) has an ammonia smell

This is caused by not enough airflow. Adjust your aging space to allow more fresh air to your cheeses, and flip it more frequently.

Aged bloomy rind cheese oozing more than I want it to

Bloomy rind cheeses can be made to have a more stable interior by either replacing part of the milk with cream (this is done for double cream and triple cream Brie), or by using washed curd technique. Eating bloomy cheeses earlier rather than later will also mean less oozing.

Unwanted moulds growing on cheeses

Introduce the preferred moulds early on. Having a healthy bloomy white or blue cheese next to the new cheese can help to introduce the moulds we want before other moulds have a chance to take over. Nature abhors a vacuum and will do her best to fill it with life - this is true whether it is a newly tilled field or the surface of a new cheese.

White moulds can also be encouraged by washing the rinds every second day for the first week, by wiping them down using a cloth dipped in whey. Smelly orange moulds can be encouraged by continuing to wash in this way beyond the first week. If your aging space does not have much humidity, aging these cheeses for the first week or two in a box with the lid ajar will also help to develop the preferred moulds.

Many moulds on hard cheeses are kept in check by regularly rubbing or brushing the surface of the cheese. Rubbing in some extra salt can also help to encourage the types of moulds we do want.

"Cat's fur fungus" looks like you'd expect it to – like clumps of grey cat's fur on the cheese. This is harmless, and an indication that not enough salt has been used on the surface of the cheese. If you don't wish to use extra salt, rubbing the cheese more frequently with your hands or a cloth will help to keep this mould in check.

Too much mould growing on cheese

Decrease the humidity by flipping the cheese more frequently onto a dry wooden surface, and allowing more airflow. Rubbing often, either with a dry cloth, or with with salt or vinegar will also help.

Not enough mould growing on cheese

Increase the humidity for a week or two by placing the cheese on a rack in a box with the lid slightly ajar, or by rubbing it with a cloth dipped in salted whey every second day for the first week. Some times of year in some aging setups can mean less mould. I just enjoy the seasonal variations of less mould on the summer cheeses and more mould at other times of year.

Craters on the surface of cheese and lots of dust around

This is probably cheese mites, which are tiny insects that eat cheese moulds. The cheese is still safe to eat, and there's actually at least one traditional cheese (French Mimolette) that encourages these mites. To discourage them, brush cheeses more frequently, and if possible, take your cheeses out of the aging space while you're brushing them. If mites are causing problems in your clothbound cheddars, mix food-grade diatomaceous earth with the lard used for clothbinding.

The cheese isn't turning out as I want it to

Many of the cheeses we're familiar with have been created by the conditions that are best in a certain place – the animals and what they are eating, the aging area, the character of the people making the cheese, and many other factors that are sometimes called "terroir". Sometimes it just isn't possible to exactly replicate a particular cheese at home, and what we can make from the milk we can access and the aging conditions is something very different, we could even be creating something very special and unique of our own.

If you are trying to make a particular cheese and it doesn't work out, don't despair – try other recipes, see what works best for you, and feel free to experiment with new techniques and do things differently to create something that's your own.

Sometimes some cheeses will work better at some times of year and not others, so it can be worthwhile to keep notes, and find out when you had trouble with a particular cheese. Patterns can emerge that in certain kinds of weather there are some issues (e.g. cheeses getting too acidic on hot days, when the kefir starter has been over-cultured, or cheeses having trouble knitting together on cold days), so that you'll know in future which cheeses are best to try on which days, and if you're trying to make a particular cheese on a less-than-ideal day, what steps can be taken to avoid these troubles.

Appendix B: Basic quick reference sheet for making a hard cheese

1. Cleaning and preparing

Clean, and optionally use boiling water to sterilise the cheese pot, rennet diluting jar, measuring spoons, thermometer, and slotted spoon.

2. Culturing

Gently pour the milk into the pot, warm it to the required temperature (usually 32°C/90°F). Gently and thoroughly mix through the culture. Let it sit at this same temperature, usually for 30 to 60 minutes. Culture is usually 1/4 cup (60ml) of kefir for 1 gallon (4 litres) milk.

3. Rennetting

Make sure the temperature is as close to 32°C (90°F) as possible. Put the pot on a stable surface where it won't be moved for the next hour. Pour a quarter cup (60ml) of unchlorinated water into a jar, add to the water as much rennet as the recipe calls for (usually ¼ tablet dry, 1/32 teaspoon powdered, or ¼ teaspoon liquid per gallon (4 litres) of milk) and stir to mix. Gently pour the diluted rennet over the top of the cultured milk, pouring it through the slotted spoon. Calmly stir the pot with the slotted spoon in an up and down motion, moving up and down in every part of the pot to distribute the rennet for one minute. Remove the spoon and thermometer and leave the pot alone for 10 to 60 minutes, or whatever the recipe says. Smaller curds tend to be cut early, larger curds later.

4. Cutting curds

Optionally sterilise your curd knife or whisk in boiling water. Check for a clean break by inserting the knife or a clean finger diagonally into the cheese, and then bringing it up vertically. If breaks apart cleanly and not in tiny pieces, then it's ready to cut. Slice the curd according to recipe directions (usually half an inch to one inch (1cm to 2cm)), and then cut these slices into squares the same size. Tilt the knife diagonally and slice into the curds as horizontally as possible, to try and create cubes all the same size. Allow to rest for five minutes.

5. Stirring and heating curds

Add back in the slotted spoon and the thermometer. From this point onwards, recipes can vary a lot. Basically, you just need to slowly and gently heat the curds to the required temperature while stirring at least every five minutes. If any curds are larger than others, break them up with a clean hand, to help them release whey at the same rate as the other curds.

Some recipes will have additional steps, beyond stirring and heating, so follow the exact recipes for details of this.

6. Pressing

Optionally sterilise your cheesecloth, cheese mould and follower in boiling water. Allow to cool, then dip your cheesecloth into the cheese pot to coat it in whey.

Test the curds to see if they are ready – they should be firm with a slight spring to them.

Place the cheesecloth in the cheese mould, trying to avoid large wrinkles. Allow the curds in the pot to settle, drain the whey into a bowl or some jars, then use your hands or the slotted spoon to put the curds in the cheesecloth.

Wrap the cheesecloth around the cheese, trying to avoid large wrinkles and dips. Press for 20 to 30 minutes according to recipe directions, flip, and press again according the recipe directions.

7. Salting

Most cheeses are now dry salted by rubbing roughly 1 tablespoon unrefined salt on the surface for every gallon (4 litres) milk.

8. Airing

Allow your cheese to air in a cool place with plenty of airflow, flipping over at least twice per day, until the surface appears dry and a rind has begun to form, usually 24-48 hours.

9. Aging

Move your small batch cheese to cool and humid place and allow to age for at last three weeks, flipping over often in the early stages of aging and moving to a dry spot each time.

Appendix C: Rennet and culture doses for larger cheeses

Kefir, whey, and other liquid cultures for any cheese:
- 120ml (half a cup) for 8 to 10 litres (2 to 2 1/2 gallons) milk.

- 240ml (1 cup) for 16 to 20 litres (4 to 5 gallons) milk.

Standard rennet dose for most cheeses:
- 1/2 tablet rennet, 1/16 teaspoon powdered rennet, or 1/2 teaspoon liquid rennet for 8 to 10 litres (2 to 2 1/2 gallons) milk.

- 1 tablet rennet, 1/8 teaspoon powdered rennet, or 1 teaspoon liquid rennet for 16 to 20 litres (4 to 5 gallons) milk.

Large rennet dose for Tomme, Alpine, and Parmesan-style cheeses:
- 3/4 tablet rennet, 1/12 teaspoon powdered rennet, or 3/4 teaspoon liquid rennet for 8 to 10 litres (2 to 2 1/2 gallons) milk.

- 1 1/2 tablets rennet, 1/6 teaspoon powdered rennet, or 1 1/2 teaspoons liquid rennet for a 16 to 20 litres (4 to 5 gallons) milk.

Vinegar for ricotta, paneer, and fast mozzarella:
- 120ml (1/2 cup) for 4 litres (1 gallon) milk.
- 180ml (3/4 cup) for 6 litres (6 quarts) milk.
- 240ml (1 cup) for 8 litres (2 gallons) milk.

Appendix D: Cheese Diary Example

Date made:_____ Date tasted:_____

Milk used:_____

Recipe name:_____

Variations from recipe:_____

_____

_____

Culture time:_____

Rennet time and temperature:_____

Curds cut:_____

Other steps:_____

_____

Heated to:_____

First press:_____

Second press:_____

Additional pressings:_____

_____

Notes:_____

_____

_____

_____

Index

Aging cheeses - 59, 60, 61, 62, 63, 100, 103, 105, 131
Airing - 58
Alpine cheese - 100, **101**, 102
Bloomy white cheeses - 81, 82, 104, 106, 108
Blue cheese - 110, 111
Brie - 106
Brined cheeses - 88
Brunost - 118
Butter - 123
Caerphilly - 112, 114
Camembert - 106, 108
Cheddar - 112, **113**, 114
Cheddaring - 52, 112, 114
Cheesecloth - 32
Cheesemaking Equipment - 32, 33, 34, 35, 36, **37**
Chèvre - **76**, 77, 78
Clabber - 75
Clean break - 44, 45, **46**
Clothbinding - 64
Coagulation - 20, 21, 22, 39, 44, 45, 46, 127, 128
Cooking curds - 49, 100, **101**, 102
Cream cheese - 77, 78
Crème fraiche - 123
Crottin - 81
Cultures - 27, 28, 29, 30, 39, 43, 44
Custard - 124
Cutting curds - 47, **48**
Draining whey - 52
Emmental - 100, **101**, 102
Farmers cheese - 75
Feta - 88, **89**, 90
Fromage blanc - 77
Ghee - 124
Gjetost - 118
Gouda - 97, 98
Gorgonzola - 111

Gruyère - 100, 102
Halloumi - 92
Havarti - **97**, 98
Herbs and spices - 57, 58, 82, 96, **97**
Hygiene - 17, 18, 19, 42, 126, 132
Ice cream - 125
Kefir - 27, 120
Labneh - 74
Leaf wrapped cheeses - 65, 83
Milk choice - 11, 12, 13, 14, 15, 129
Milk handling - 16, 18, 19,
Moulds - 63, 64, 104, 105, 110, 111, 132, 133
Mountain cheese - 100, **101**, 102
Mozzarella - 84, 86, 129, 130
Mysost - 118
Oiling rinds - 64
Paneer - 72
Parmesan - 116
Problems - 126, 127, 128, 129, 130, 131, 132
Pressing cheese - 35, 40, 53, **54**, **55**, 130
Quark - 75
Rennet - 20, 21, 22, 39, 44, 45, 46, 127, 128
Rennet, homemade - 23, 24, 25, 26
Ricotta - 72, 117
Ripening - 27, 28, 29, 30, 39, 43, 44
Salt - 31, 40, 56,
Stirring curds - 49
Sour cream - 123
Testing curds - 49, **50**, **51**
Tomme - 94
Valençay - ladled curd chèvre, 82
Vegetable ash - 57
Washing curds - 51, 96, 98, 99
Waxing cheeses - 64
Whey - 68, 69, 117
Yoghurt - 120, 121, 122, 123
Yoghurt cheese - 74

www.ingramcontent.com/pod-product-compliance
Lightning Source LLC
Chambersburg PA
CBHW051157290426
44109CB00022B/2495